More COFFEE SHOP THEOLOGY

TRANSLATING DOCTRINAL JARGON INTO EVERYDAY LIFE

FRANK MOORE

Beacon Hill Press of Kansas City
Kansas City, Missouri

Copyright 1998
by Beacon Hill Press of Kansas City

ISBN 083-411-7460

Printed in the
United States of America

Cover Design: Mike Walsh
Cover Illustration: Keith Alexander

Library of Congress Cataloging-in-Publication Data
Moore, Frank, 1951-
   More coffee shop theology : translating doctrinal jargon into everyday life / Frank Moore.
     p. cm.
   Includes bibligraphical references.
   ISBN 0-8341-1746-0 (pbk.)
   1. Theology, Doctrinal—Popular works. I. Title.
BT77.M824   1998   98-25705
230—dc21   CIP

10 9 8 7 6 5 4 3 2 1

To Brent,
the best son a dad
could ask for.
I hope this book helps
pass the faith from
my generation to yours.

CONTENTS

CHRISTIAN LIFE

LAST THINGS

PREFACE

Welcome. Or, welcome back. I give both greetings because this is the continuation of a story I began in another book, titled *Coffee Shop Theology*. Both volumes are my attempt, as the subtitle says, to translate our Christian faith into concepts that apply to everyday life.

Most readers will pick up this volume after having read *Coffee Shop Theology*. But, I am aware that it is possible that someone might pick this book up first. Therefore, I have done something very unusual. In fact, I've never seen it done quite this way before. Breaking our discussion in the middle like we have done creates a problem. *Coffee Shop Theology* concluded with a discussion of the resurrection of Jesus Christ. Our next topic of discussion centers around the salvation God provides for us. However, if a reader picks this book up and begins to read here first, God's plan of salvation cannot be understood without understanding the life, ministry, death, and resurrection of Jesus Christ.

Therefore, my editor and I have decided to begin this volume by reprinting the five chapters discussing Jesus Christ. If you happen to be reading this book without having read *Coffee Shop Theology*, these chapters on Jesus will give you a running start into our subject matter. I would suggest you go ahead and read this book now, and read *Coffee Shop Theology* later. Or, if it has been awhile since you read the former volume, I would urge you to reread the chapters on Jesus to refresh your memory on His wonderful life and work. It will add new insight to our discussion of God's salvation plan.

If, on the other hand, you are picking this book up after having recently read *Coffee Shop Theology*, then I'd say you might wish to skip the Introduction and the first five chapters. Either way, let's get started.

INTRODUCTION

MORE COFFEE SHOP THEOLOGY

I'm excited about the subject matter of this book. Theology consumes me as the central interest of my life; I live, breathe, and talk it every day. I'm excited because it's a brand-new day for theology. More than ever before, we Christians must know what we believe and why. The reason is simple but serious:

> *If our anchor isn't set in a solid rock theology, we'll be washed out to sea on the riptide of bogus beliefs.*

We are bombarded with an information revolution. We access more information in less time than any generation in human history. Thousands of pages of information come to us on one computer compact disk. A keystroke or two on our computers gets us into the Internet, which provides access to information from around the world. Fax machines, electronic mail, cellular telephones, television, radio, magazines, satellite, cable, and other technologies make our world smaller and bring us closer together. As one of my friends compared it, "We're trying to drink out of a fire hydrant."

The information in this book goes beyond facts and figures; it's ethics, philosophy, and theology all packaged in innocent bite-size (or *byte*-size) portions.

What is all this information doing to us? One serious consequence is *rapidly changing cultural standards that encourage us to bargain away our beliefs.* We now have a cafeteria line of beliefs. Modern society cherishes pluralism more each day. This approach welcomes all systems of thought as equally true, regardless of how unscriptural they may be or how strange they may sound. It says that none is better or worse. Absolute truth evaporates like the morning dew in this environment. Everyone's ideas claim validity as possible answers to our most pressing questions.

Such so-called tolerance and acceptance create theological uncertainty, in which all answers are tentative, in which people will clap for any idea on a television talk show. Everything, especially sound doctrine based on Holy Scripture, is up for grabs these days. If you don't believe me, read the articles in recent newspapers or newsmagazines about the unprecedented success of outlandish cults. *The stranger their beliefs, the quicker people line up and pay good money to join.* Hollywood stars trip over one another to be deceived. Where can we find truth these days?

One of the marks of Christianity, from the times of the Early Church until now, is its claim to God's truth. The Truth—not *a* truth. The Christian faith is not just a better idea equal to all other ideas. Christianity contends that God answers the most basic questions of human existence:

Who am I?
Where did I come from?
Why am I here?
What does my life mean?
Where am I going?

These questions finally relate to establishing an incredibly significant friendship with God. Christian believers through the ages have hungered to know Him better.

Never has this quest for God been as widespread as it is now. My grandparents lived a full life and died without ever having come in contact with individuals practicing another world religion. That is no longer true. We come in contact with followers of non-Christian religions every time we step outside, listen to the radio, watch a television program, or read the newspaper. Even if we stay home and never turn on the radio or television, faithful followers of these other religions will knock on our door, offering to instruct us in their ways. Their hospitality often rivals that of the welcome wagon.

Another reason Christians must more thoroughly understand their faith is because contemporary values do not hold the answers to our deepest questions. Science and technology have promised more than they have been able to deliver. We are giving up on those empty promises, because their answers don't work in life's trenches. Thus, as people continue their search for meaning and significance, they seem more willing to hear what the Christian faith offers.

So we have a two-part reason to understand our Christian faith more completely and accurately:

(1) to satisfy our own hungry souls;
(2) to be able to offer God's answers to friends whose questions about life and death push into their waking thoughts and sleepless nights.

C. S. Lewis made an insightful observation: "In the old days, where there was less education and discussion, perhaps it was possible to get on with a very few simple ideas about God. But it is not so now. Everyone reads, everyone hears things discussed. Consequently, if you do not listen to Theology, that will now mean that you have no ideas about God. It will mean that you have a lot of wrong ones—bad, muddled, out-of-date ideas."[1] Thus, we seek to understand our faith as completely and accurately as we can.

Concerning this journey of faith, I intend to present an easy-to-understand and true-to-life use of theology. Please don't get out the Pepto-Bismol or Tylenol if I sometimes end an explanation by calling it a mystery. By "mystery" I simply mean that human minds cannot completely comprehend God's ways. *Our inability to fully understand does not leave us completely in the dark nor make God unknowable or unreasonable.* Therefore, when I acknowledge a mystery, it's not a cop-out, but a human limitation. Because God is infinite, our finite minds can never understand His wisdom. God is Creator; we are created. Big difference!

Knowing God better satisfies our hunger and creates more hunger. It satisfies us at a deep level because our hearts find rest in Him. At the same time, we hunger to know more. On the pages of this book I try to communicate Christianity's central truths with simplicity, clarity, and brevity.

As I write these words, I picture us discussing these issues over a cup of coffee at the café on Main Street in my little hometown. The older men of the community gathered there during my childhood to discuss weather, politics, and religion. They sat for hours and thrashed out solutions. Most of the problems of the world could have been solved in short order if world leaders would have visited that café and heeded those men's advice! *So read this work in the context of a friendly discussion at that little café.*

The topics, Bible references, quotes, and applications to life aim to inform and inspire your faith. The "Biblical Foundation" section of each chapter offers biblical references and includes basic truths that are all found in the life and ministry of Jesus Christ. I worked hard to discuss the realities of faith in understandable language so anyone can apply them to life. I left all the big words in the fat books. This exercise of stating the miraculous work of God in plain speech has stimulated my own faith and excited me about its utter simplicity. We have an incredible message from God! I hope these discussions excite you as well.

Each of these short chapters presents a different aspect of our faith. However, the topics are interrelated like links of a chain, so I make connections between them from time to time. They all work together to form a whole picture. Note that the longest section of material discusses our salvation. That is because salvation is the main focus of Christianity and the chief message of Scripture. All doctrines feed into a better understanding of our salvation. Christlikeness, heaven, and fellowship with God are the ultimate goals.

I hope you enjoy reading through this journey as much as I did writing it. I don't intend for you to make your way through it in one setting. A better plan is to read a chapter each day in your devotional time. Read a chapter, and then think about its application to your life throughout the day. Ask the Holy Spirit to give you new insights. I believe we will become more Christlike as we walk through our faith daily down Main Street. So let's order a cup of coffee and a soft chocolate-chip cookie and get started.

JESUS CHRIST

The whole question of the virgin birth of Jesus need not afflict the average man. If Jesus is unique, unlike any other person, it is not illogical to believe that his birth was unique.
—William Lyon Phelps

CHAPTER 1

JESUS' MYSTERIOUS ARRIVAL

THE VIRGIN CONCEPTION

Biblical Foundation

"Therefore the Lord himself will give you a sign: The virgin will be with child and will give birth to a son, and will call him Immanuel" (Isa. 7:14).

"This is how the birth of Jesus Christ came about: His mother Mary was pledged to be married to Joseph, but before they came together, she was found to be with child through the Holy Spirit. Because Joseph her husband was a righteous man and did not want to expose her to public disgrace, he had in mind to divorce her quietly. But after he had considered this, an angel of the Lord appeared to him in a dream and said, 'Joseph son of David, do not be afraid to take Mary home as your wife, because what is conceived in her is from the Holy Spirit'" (Matt. 1:18-20).

Jesus never tried to defend His unique origin. No doubt as a child He heard the rumors as people discussed His arrival shortly after His parents' wedding. Such subjects interested people then as they do today. So why did He not address the issue? Probably because He could offer no reasonable explanation for Mary's virgin conception. The Bible states it as God's plan, and that's that.

The Truth Explained in Everyday Language

Our extended family gathers around the jigsaw puzzle table every Christmas holiday to assemble a new puzzle. It's a Christmas tradition. Brent and my mother-in-law find it challenging, relaxing, and fun. Everyone gathers and relaxes except me; I find puzzles frustrating and nerve-racking. The puzzle pieces supposedly fit together, forming a coherent picture—but I can't seem to make any of the pieces fit where they belong. I try to force pieces together, but they refuse to cooperate. Finally I leave the table and forget it.

Some find the Christian doctrine of the Virgin Birth just as frustrating. The Bible gives us a variety of factual statements surrounding the earthly arrival of Jesus Christ. We desperately attempt to make the statements reasonably fit together. When they don't fit as we would like, we can become frustrated and deny scriptural truth or give up on the entire matter. A better strategy studies biblical statements and accepts them at face value. Faith and an awareness of our limited human reason help. We must refuse to accept only reasonable answers.

The doctrine is historically known as the Virgin Birth. Actually, virgin *conception* more accurately represents it, since the conception and not the birth is under consideration. The prophet Isaiah announced several hundred years before Jesus' arrival that the Messiah would be conceived of a virgin (7:14). Gospel writers Matthew and Luke document the only accounts of the announcement and birth of Jesus; both present the virgin conception of Jesus (Matt. 1:18-25; Luke 1:26-38).

Matthew approaches the matter from Joseph's perspective, while Luke presents Mary's view. Only Mary and Joseph, the two key figures in the event, had firsthand knowledge. Both of them staked their reputations on a story without logical explanation. If they intended to lie, they should have created a more reasonable story than this one. You don't make up outlandish stories like this. In deciding between truth and reason, they chose truth, regardless of the consequences.

God miraculously conceived Jesus in Mary's body. She had no sexual activity either with man or God. While sexual activity between human and divine beings commonly occurred in ancient mythology, it has no place in this account. Mary carried her first child to full term as any other mother. She birthed Him in a natural way. Some Christians believe in a miraculous delivery without use of the birth canal, but the Bible nowhere teaches this. These Christians also believe that Mary remained a virgin throughout her life. The Bible teaches otherwise, stating that Jesus had both brothers and sisters who were no doubt conceived naturally (Matt. 13:55-56; Mark 6:3).

Some critics of the Matthew and Luke accounts argue that none of the other Gospel writers knew about the virgin conception—that they would have written about it had they known. Not necessarily. Mark wrote an abbreviated account of the life and ministry of Jesus and did not have room to include a birth account. John's Gospel addressed theological issues, not personal matters in Christ's life. The other New Testament books focused on specific practical or theological questions as they arose in the Early Church. None of them offered details about Jesus' personal life. The absence in other books of a discussion of Jesus' conception does not imply an error in Matthew and Luke. The fact may have been so accepted in that day that biblical writers saw no reason to restate it.

A couple of references in Mark and John may hint that some believed Jesus was illegitimate. People in that day no doubt calculated the time between Mary and Joseph's marriage and Jesus' birth as readily as they do today. They knew the time was too short. Thus, there may be an implied insult when the Jews defended themselves to Jesus by reminding Him that *they* were not illegitimate, as He had been accused of being (John 8:41). Commonly in biblical times, a young man was identified as the son of his father. Yet in Mark 6:3, the hometown crowds referred to Jesus as "Mary's son." Perhaps His earthly father was dead, or perhaps they believed that Jesus was illegitimate and had no legal father.

The Early Church never doubted the virgin conception of Jesus.

Jesus Christ came to earth as a man but remained the Son of God, the Second Member of the Trinity. In order to demonstrate His uniqueness, God chose an unusual method for His conception. In other words, He did not come to earth in the natural way. Some people attempt to connect this doctrine to the doctrine of original sin and say Jesus had no original sin because Mary had no sexual intercourse. From this they deduce that sex creates sinfulness, that sexual intercourse is sinful, or that the male genes contain original sin. This has given many people a very negative impression of sexual activity between husbands and wives. Never. God ordained sexual expression as a high and holy physical and spiritual bond between husbands and wives. Jesus' virgin conception casts no shadows upon God's plan for sex in marriage.

The Early Church never doubted the virgin conception of Jesus. It became an accepted fact of early Christian tradition. The Apostles' Creed, one of the early statements of Christian faith, includes an affirmation of the virgin conception. Only in modern times have Christians doubted this important doctrine.

The chief doubt centers on conflict with reason. It isn't natural, so some people refuse to accept it. However, since God rules sovereignly over everything in heaven and earth, He can do anything He wants to do. Since He is all-powerful, He can work any type of miracle He wants. Our understanding in no way binds Him in accomplishing His purposes. As Grandma always said, "All things are possible with God." He chose to send His Son to earth through a virgin, and that's a fact.

Using the Truth to Enrich Your Life

What connection does this doctrine have to life? An important one indeed. For more than a century now, this doctrine has been used as a test case to see if Christians can accept the miracle-working power of God, the divine nature of Christ, and the miraculous nature of our salvation. If they cannot accept this doctrine, then chances are they won't accept the other divine elements of our faith either.

———

**If I can accept my salvation
as a miracle of God's grace,
then I must also believe
He can work gracious miracles
in other ways as well.**

God sometimes works through natural processes, but He sometimes performs miracles. He sometimes makes things simple and easy for us to understand, but He sometimes asks us to lay our reason aside and let Him blow our circuits. If I can accept my salvation as a miracle of God's grace, then I must also believe He can work gracious miracles in other ways as well. I cannot understand it, but I don't doubt the truth of God's Word when it reveals His plan.

Fast Takes

1. God sent His Son to earth through a virgin conception.
2. The virgin conception is a clearly established fact of Scripture and church history.
3. Acceptance of the fact of the virgin conception takes faith and an awareness of limited human reason.

Prayer

Thank You, Father, for the miracle of Christ's conception. Help me trust Your incomprehensible plan of salvation.

Jesus Christ is the best picture God ever took.
—Little girl in Sunday School class

CHAPTER 2

GOD WITH US

THE DEITY OF CHRIST

Biblical Foundation

"Simon Peter answered, 'You [Jesus] are the Christ, the Son of the living God'" (Matt. 16:16).

"The Word became flesh and made his dwelling among us. We have seen his glory, the glory of the One and Only, who came from the Father, full of grace and truth" (John 1:14).

The New Testament contains many evidences of Jesus' divinity. His conception by the Father, His miracles, His powerful ministry, His incredible love, His resurrection from the dead, His ascension back to the Father—all testified to His deity. People argue against the evidence, but they cannot disprove it.

The Truth Explained in Everyday Language

Christianity clearly affirms Christ's divinity. If it is true, we have the greatest message ever told. If not, He was a con artist and we have no hope. The deity of Christ literally leaps from the pages of the Bible, giving us evidence that demands a verdict. Augustine summarized it best when he declared, "Christ is not valued at all—unless He is valued above all."[1]

Jesus acknowledged His divinity during His earthly ministry but did not proclaim it openly, not wishing to antagonize His enemies prematurely. Yet He dropped hints of His deity throughout His ministry. He said He was one with the Father (John 10:30). He told Philip that anyone who had seen Him had seen the Father (14:9-10). When people questioned His divine status, Jesus urged them to examine His miracles and ministry as proof of who He said He was (10:37-38). When asked at His trial before the Jewish Sanhedrin, "Are you then the Son of God?" He replied, "You are right in saying I am" (Luke 22:70).

Jesus' disciples spent more than three years with Him. They knew Him as well as anyone, and they recognized His divinity. In his great confession, Simon Peter proclaimed Jesus as the long-awaited Christ (Matt. 16:16). John said Jesus lived with the Father prior to the creation of the world and actually helped create and sustain all things (John 1:1-3). The apostle Paul stated in Col. 2:9, "In Christ all the fullness of the Deity lives in bodily form." Hebrews refers to Jesus as "the radiance of God's glory and the exact representation of his being" (1:3) and said He was superior to angels, Moses, and high priests (chaps. 1; 3; 4—5). Even the evil spirits whom Jesus rebuked in His ministry acknowledged His deity (Matt. 8:29; Mark 1:24; 3:11; Luke 4:41). It's really saying something when your enemies testify for you!

Several statements from Jesus' ministry affirmed His divinity. For example, He existed prior to His birth on earth. "'I tell you the truth,' Jesus answered, 'before Abraham was born, I am!'" (John 8:58). He even existed prior to the creation of the world: "And now, Father, glorify me in your presence with the glory I had with you before the world began" (17:5). He amazed the crowds with His authority. "When Jesus had finished saying these things, the crowds were amazed at his teaching, because he taught as one who had authority, and not as their teachers of the law" (Matt. 7:28-29). (See also Matt. 28:18; Mark 1:27; John 5:27.)

———

Something about Jesus' take-charge attitude convinced the disciples of His authority.

Jesus further amazed the crowds and His disciples with His awareness of events before they happened. The Bible documents several instances. For example, He knew that the religious leaders of the day would reject Him and His teachings (Mark 8:31). He knew that Judas would betray Him (John 13:11). He recognized His time to return to the Father (16:5). He knew He would die with common criminals (Luke 22:37).

Something about Jesus' take-charge attitude convinced the disciples of His authority. On one occasion, when the Pharisees confronted Him for breaking religious laws by picking grain from a field and eating it, He said, "The Son of Man is Lord of the Sabbath" (Luke 6:5). On another occasion He angered the Pharisees for healing a man with a shriveled right hand on the Sabbath. Here He asked, "Which is lawful on the Sabbath: to do good or to do evil, to save life or to destroy it?" (v. 9). He then healed the man's hand—to the great displeasure of the Pharisees. Of course, they didn't approve of anything He did. He couldn't boil water to suit them. The disciples never got over the time He calmed a storm on the Sea of Galilee. They asked, "What kind of man is this? Even the winds and the waves obey him!" (Matt. 8:27).

Doubters throughout church history have denied the deity of Christ. The mystery defies humankind's reason since their human brains cannot contain divine ways. So they deny them. Some said He was just an ordinary man with unusual intelligence and understanding. Others said He could not be divine because that would divide God into two beings. They taught He was created just as angels and all living things on the earth, thus there was a time when He did not exist. The Christian community rejects these and all other denials of Christ's deity. C. S. Lewis leaves no option: "A man who was merely a man and said the sort of things Jesus said would not be a great moral teacher. He would either be a lunatic—on a level with the man who says he is a poached egg—or else he would be the Devil of Hell. You can shut Him up for a fool, you can spit at Him and kill Him as a demon; or you can fall at His feet and call Him Lord and God."[2]

Using the Truth to Enrich Your Life

Heroes are in short supply these days. I'm not talking about cartoon characters or television stars; I'm talking about real people who represent the best and the highest principles of life. Media and sports celebrities abound, but not many heroes. Celebrities have name recognition; heroes have moral character. Heroes are important because they uphold a high example and urge us to be our best.

**Jesus Christ represents
the greatest hero
the world has ever seen.**

Jesus Christ represents the greatest hero the world has ever seen. Everything He said and everything He did reflected the best and highest principles of life. We can pattern our lives after His. That was one of His purposes in coming to earth—to give us an example, to start us on the path of Christlikeness. He taught us to love everyone, turn the other cheek, forgive those who hurt us, be patient, be longsuffering, be kind, and to exhibit a host of other qualities. His example not only demonstrated what God expects of us but also demonstrated what God himself is like. He lived perfectly because He was divine. His actions came from no script, but rather from the habits of His heart.

So the next time you're in the market for a hero, look to Jesus Christ—the best picture God ever took.

Fast Takes

1. Jesus Christ is divine.
2. Jesus' disciples knew Him best, and they affirmed His divinity.
3. Everything about Jesus' life and ministry supported His claim to divinity.
4. Human doubt does not change the fact of Christ's divinity.

Prayer

Father, our lives have been enriched by the clear picture of You given to us through Christ. He is our Hero.

Jesus came to us to become as we are and left us to allow us to become as he is.

—Henri Nouwen

CHAPTER 3

A PERSONAL VISIT FROM THE BOSS

THE HUMANITY OF CHRIST

Biblical Foundation

> *"For there is one God and one mediator between God and men, the man Christ Jesus"* (1 Tim. 2:5).

> *"Beyond all question, the mystery of godliness is great: He appeared in a body, was vindicated by the Spirit, was seen by angels, was preached among the nations, was believed on in the world, was taken up in glory"* (1 Tim. 3:16).

Jesus grew up in a family with responsibilities, worked a job, and lived with His disciples just as any other human being. He got hungry, thirsty, and tired just as we do. The Bible gives us the highs and lows from the life of Jesus that paint the picture of a very human individual. Some people see only His divinity, but this is not a biblical picture.

The Truth Explained in Everyday Language

I worked on a highway construction crew every summer during my college years. The days were long, and the work was hard. Most of the roads we worked on were in the mountainous northern part of the state. The company owner lived in the center of the state. It took several hours for him to drive to our work sites to check on construction progress. So he didn't come very often; he usually sent his son to check on things.

I'll never forget the difference in the way I reacted to the visits of the company owner in contrast to those of his son. The owner maintained the presence of a rich and powerful man. He dressed like a million dollars and could fire you with a word. Every worker at the work site, especially me, tensed up when he paid us a visit. The owner's son left the opposite impression when he came. His relaxed dress and manner put everyone at ease. He wasn't much older than me, so I readily identified with him. I talked with him the way I talked with my coworkers. We much preferred his visits to his father's.

The humanity of Jesus gave us a flesh-and-blood picture of God, an insider's perspective.

For some reason people in Old Testament times grew to fear God in much the same way as we feared our company owner. I don't mean a healthy reverence or respect—I mean *scared to death* of Him. Look at how the Israelites reacted when God invited them to join Moses at Mount Sinai to receive the Ten Commandments. They refused to go near the mountain. They told Moses to go alone (Exod. 20:18-21). That is fairly characteristic of the way most people felt about God throughout the Old Testament. Perhaps the voices from the bushes, the smoking mountains, and the fiery clouds scared them.

Jesus' coming changed all that. God didn't change; rather, our perception of Him did. The humanity of Jesus gave us a flesh-and-blood picture of God, an insider's perspective. We no longer need to guess how God feels about us. Like a singing telegram, Jesus brought us warm, personal greetings from the Father. As George Hodges put it, "We know what God is like because we know the character of Jesus Christ."[1]

When Jesus came to earth, He identified fully with us. He had a physical body and experienced normal physical limitations like hunger, thirst, and fatigue. He grew up in a normal family structure with parents and siblings. History speculates that Joseph died during Jesus' teenage years. If so, Jesus assumed added family responsibility at an early age.

Jesus had a human psychological and emotional makeup and experienced the full range of human emotions. He knew happy times and sad, good times and bad, successful days and failure. Perhaps some of His greatest frustration with failure came from trying to instruct His disciples in God's ways, only to have them misunderstand His message time after time. Would they ever get it right? They seemed so thickheaded. But I don't judge them; I'm not so sure I would have caught on any quicker. He experienced the stress of a hectic schedule with long hours of ministry and travel. He also dealt with personality conflict in working with the Pharisees and Sadducees. It was like trying to mix water and oil when they got together.

Jesus also had a normal human religious life. He attended worship services with His parents as a child and continued the practice throughout His adult life. He and His disciples always participated in public worship on the Sabbath and special religious days. He was baptized in a normal fashion and participated in all the religious festivals and rites of the day. He prayed often with the Father and depended upon Him in every area of His life. He fulfilled all the expected religious practices of the day and modeled exemplary behavior in His religious life.

Phil. 2:6-7 gives helpful insight into the humanity of Christ: "Who, being in very nature God, did not consider equality with God something to be grasped, but made himself nothing, taking the very nature of a servant, being made in human likeness." What did Jesus give up in making himself nothing when He assumed human form? Some think He gave up His divinity or the use of His divine abilities. Others think He only pretended to be limited by His humanity. Jesus indeed was limited by His body and all that bound Him to the earth. He did not fly or defeat His enemies like Superman. He gave up independent use of His divine abilities and became totally dependent upon the Father in His ministry and miracles. That's why He lived so close to the Father and prayed so much.

Some teach that Jesus did not actually have a human body, because they believe the physical body and earthly matter are infected with evil. To their way of thinking, Jesus could not be divine with an earthly body. They solve this problem by saying He only *seemed* to have a body. In other words, He was a phantom or a very good hologram. Others err by teaching that the divine Jesus wore a human body the way we wear clothes. By denying Jesus a human nature, they deny full identification with us and a human will. These beliefs are all wrong. Jesus had a normal human body, just like ours. He experienced the aches and pains of life just as we do. He also had a human nature and a divine nature at the same time. He was not 50 percent God and 50 percent man in some schizophrenic manner. Rather, He was 100 percent of both at the same time. This is another mystery of faith but true nonetheless—another circuit breaker.

One of the biggest questions surrounding Jesus' humanity is "Could He sin?" My students love to debate this. If He was fully divine with a divine nature, then the answer is no—God cannot sin. If His temptations were live options appealing to His human nature, then the answer is yes. If we take Heb. 4:15 seriously, the answer has to be yes: "For we do not have a high priest who is unable to sympathize with our weaknesses, but we have one who has been *tempted in every way, just as we are*—yet was without sin" (emphasis added.) Scholars have debated the question for centuries without a resolution. Both positions have equally valid biblical arguments. Give it some personal reflection time; see what you decide. Perhaps the best response is to acknowledge that He *could* have sinned because of His humanity, but He *would not* because of His divinity.

Using the Truth to Enrich Your Life

Many of my adult students work for companies that require their executives to spend time on the front line with the common workers. They answer the phone, work the assembly line, or make business calls with coworkers. This gives them a personal identity with their employees and keeps them current with operating procedures. The executives get firsthand exposure to the stresses and strains of the job. They understand the company from the bottom up. My students find the practice helpful.

**When we unburden our hearts
with the matters that concern us,
He not only listens
but also fully understands.**

Jesus made the ultimate executive visit; the Creator came to live with His creatures. He spent time on the front line of life in a way that we'll never fully understand. He personally identified with us, was tempted with the things that tempt us, and was stressed by the things that stress us. He experienced life just as we do. The good news is that He remained victorious. He did not sin or fail the test of life.

This realization makes prayer so much more meaningful. When we unburden our hearts with the matters that concern us, He not only listens but also fully understands. When we sense Him saying, "I know what you're going through," He really does. He can honestly say, "I've been there." When we're tempted to our limits, we can call on Him for strength and power. He maintained victory over His temptations, and so can we. He lived a victorious life, and so can we—with the help of an expert. He has the winner's edge. We don't have to go it alone; God gives us the best help possible—help from personal experience.

Fast Takes

1. The humanity of Jesus gives us a flesh-and-blood picture of God.

2. God did not change from the Old Testament, but our perception of Him changed as a result of Jesus.
3. Jesus experienced the full range of needs and limitations as a human being.
4. By identifying with us, Jesus fully understands our situation.

Prayer

Jesus, thank You for visiting us personally and showing us the way back to the Father.

The Cross is the only ladder high enough to touch heaven's threshold.

—G. D. Boardman

CHAPTER 4

A COVERING FOR OUR SINS

THE ATONEMENT OF CHRIST

Biblical Foundation

"Just as man is destined to die once, and after that to face judgment, so Christ was sacrificed once to take away the sins of many people; and he will appear a second time, not to bear sin, but to bring salvation to those who are waiting for him" (Heb. 9:27-28).

"He is the atoning sacrifice for our sins, and not only for ours but also for the sins of the whole world" (1 John 2:2).

Jesus often talked about coming to earth to restore fellowship with God. He talked about giving His life as a ransom for many and dying for the sins of the world. He said His enemies could not take His life away from Him; He gave it freely. Jesus knew that when His task was accomplished, a new way to God would be open.

The Truth Explained in Everyday Language

Jesus Christ brought us a personal message from the Father and gave us an example of God's love. But He came to do much more than that; He came to die on the Cross for our sins. People in recent years have asked numerous questions about this. Here are a few of those questions:

- Why was it necessary for Him to die for us?
- What was accomplished in His death that could have been accomplished no other way?

- What is the significance of the blood of Christ for our salvation?
- For whom did Christ die?

William Tyndale, English Bible translator, could not find an adequate English word to describe what Christ did for us on the Cross. So he made one up by combining two words: "at" and "onement"; Christ brought the Holy Father and sinful humanity together through His sacrifice. C. S. Lewis summarized it by saying, "The central Christian belief is that Christ's death has somehow put us right with God and given us a fresh start."[1]

In order to understand the atonement of Christ, we must explore the Old Testament sacrificial system. God established this method of dealing with sin soon after the Fall. Explanations and examples of sacrifices offered to God abound throughout the Old Testament, especially the Book of Leviticus. People brought animals to God each year to demonstrate their sorrow for the sins committed that year. The sacrifices could not be sickly or lame animals; they had to be the best of the herd, the cream of the crop.

When presenting the animals for sacrifice, the priest symbolically prayed the sins of the people onto the animal. Then the animal died for those sins. The blood symbolized the animal's life, which was taken because of the people's disobedience to God, reminding everyone of sin's seriousness. The animal's blood atoned for, or "covered," the sins. People left the worship service hoping God accepted their sacrifice but without peace of heart or a clear conscience. The next year they repeated the ritual.

Heb. 9—10 gives the best explanation of how Jesus Christ fulfilled the Old Testament sacrificial system with His death on the Cross. In this passage we see Jesus characterized in the double role as both the Victim sacrificed and the Priest offering the sacrifice to the Father (9:11; 10:10). The shedding of Christ's blood brought forgiveness for our sins (9:22). Better than any spotless animal, Jesus was sinless (v. 14). Animal sacrifices can't really take sins away anyway (10:4). Christ's sacrifice *can* (v. 10). Also, because of His sinlessness, He did not need to make a sacrifice for himself as the priests and high priest were required to do (9:7). Because of the perfection of Christ's sacrifice, the conscience of the sinner is cleared (vv. 9, 14; 10:2). Not only are our consciences cleared, but also we are made pure and holy in God's sight (v. 14) and given an eternal inheritance in heaven (9:15). Christ's sacrifice is the last one needed in the Old Testament sacrificial system. It is perfect and complete; nothing more is ever required (10:18).

The New Testament frequently speaks of Christ's atonement. At the Last Supper with His disciples, Jesus declared, "This is my blood of the covenant, which is poured out for many for the forgiveness of sins" (Matt. 26:28). Paul reminded us in Eph. 1:7-8, "In him we have redemption through his blood, the forgiveness of sins, in accordance with the riches of God's grace that he lavished on us with all wisdom and understanding." Jesus commented of himself, "The Son of Man did not come to be served, but to serve, and to give his life as a ransom for many" (Matt. 20:28). The concept of Jesus' dying as a ransom to bring us back to God appears 140 times in the New Testament.

Many ideas throughout church history have attempted to explain how Jesus' death atoned for our sins. Each seeks to add light to our understanding of Christ's atonement. Some are more helpful than others; all have a measure of truth. When we put them together like pieces of a model airplane, we gain insight into God's wonderful plan to save us from sin.

Some people see the death of Christ as an example of God's great love for us. It shows His compassion rather than condemnation. When we see Christ hanging on the Cross, we say to ourselves, "That is how much God loves me." Others add that this demonstration of God's love should compel us to be our best for God. Christ's death influences us to do right. God believes in us, and we ought to live accordingly. Still others say the death of Christ demonstrates God's judgment on sin. While God loves us, He cannot wink at the seriousness of our sins or ignore the fact that we have broken His laws. When we see Christ hanging on the Cross, we say to ourselves, "That shows the seriousness of sin and the high cost of forgiveness." Still another idea deals with our failure to worship and honor God as we should because of sin. Christ died to give the Father the honor we failed to offer, thus satisfying our debt.

Christ's identification with us
allows Him to represent our case
before the Father.

One of the most popular ideas in modern time centers around punishment. This idea teaches that God is perfect and holy; His law reflects His nature. When we sin, we attack the nature of God and defy His character. When Christ died on the Cross, the Father laid every sin of every sinner on Him and punished Him for them. This idea has several problems. First, the New Testament seems to indicate that Jesus suffered for us, not that He was punished in our place. Next, it implies that God dispenses retributive justice as punishment in a legalistic way. It leaves no room for mercy. Finally, it satisfies the legal order or letter of the law but does not show God's great love for us.

Two other words must be added to our picture of Christ's atonement: "identify" and "represent." Jesus came to earth to identify with our sinful human condition. He suffered all of the limitations of humanness, except those involving sin. He went so far as to die for our sins. Now we can be reconciled to God by faith as we identify ourselves with Him. We accept His sacrifice for our sins, just as the Father has accepted it and no longer holds our sins against us. We are crucified with Christ, buried with Him in baptism, and raised to newness of life. His identification with us allows Him to represent our case before the Father. He becomes our Representative and stands in our behalf. God no longer remembers our sins against us; it is as if we never sinned. We can joyously sing the words of Nellie Edwards: "They are covered by the blood; / They are covered by the blood; / My sins are all covered by the blood."

Using the Truth to Enrich Your Life

People all over the world fill mental hospitals and counselors' offices seeking ways to erase their sinful pasts. Haunted by reminders of skeletons in their closets, they desperately seek a fresh, new start. Some of my friends visit counselors regularly. I have watched them pay large sums of money over long periods of time with little satisfaction. Counselors have no techniques completely able to meet this deep human need. Only Christ can bring a divine answer that works.

———

Dan became a living miracle of the power of God.

My friend Dan tried everything. He fell into the bondage of tobacco, alcohol, drugs, illicit sex, and several other vices. His life was a mess. He finally reached the end of himself and sought a way out. I urged him to try Christ. He did, and his life turned around completely. He became a brand-new person. The bondage broke; the damage of his past began to heal. His heart and mind cleared, and he experienced new freedom. He became a living miracle of the power of God. Dan and millions like him are living proof that the atonement of Christ changes lives.

Fast Takes

1. The Old Testament sacrificial system brought atonement by praying sins onto animals and sacrificing their lives.
2. Jesus Christ completed that system by making the last, perfect sacrifice—himself.
3. Christ's atonement on the Cross demonstrates God's love, compels us to live righteously, shows God's judgment on sin,

stresses the seriousness of sin, and illustrates the high cost of forgiveness.

4. We identify with Christ in His death; He represents us to the Father.

Prayer

Dear Father, I bow in humble gratitude for the high price You paid for my salvation. Help me to see a brief glimpse of Your immeasurable love for me.

Belief in the resurrection is not an appendage
to the Christian faith; it is the Christian faith.
—John S. Whale

CHAPTER 5

UP FROM THE GRAVE

THE RESURRECTION OF CHRIST

Biblical Foundation

"Christ has indeed been raised from the dead, the firstfruits of those who have fallen asleep" (1 Cor. 15:20).

"Praise be to the God and Father of our Lord Jesus Christ! In his great mercy he has given us new birth into a living hope through the resurrection of Jesus Christ from the dead" (1 Pet. 1:3).

Jesus predicted the Father would raise Him from the dead after His cruel ordeal on the Cross. It happened just as He said. He surprised His disciples when they saw Him alive. They shouldn't have been surprised. He was just keeping His word to them.

The Truth Explained in Everyday Language

Some events are so monumental that they affect the rest of our life. They become pivotal points for our personal history. Such events may be marriage, the birth of a child, a career promotion, winning a contest or award, or a variety of other things. No event in our lives, however, can compare to the impact that the resurrection of Jesus Christ had on the first-century Christians and the future of the Christian Church. As John S. Whale so wisely put it, "The Gospels do not explain the resurrection; the resurrection explains the Gospels."[1]

When Jesus died on the Cross, His disciples lost all hope and retreated in fear behind locked doors. The curtains had fallen on their hopes for God's kingdom. They awakened to new life after His resurrection, however, and even defied religious authorities. Only a divine miracle can account for such a radical transformation. This event rocked the political and religious world of the Roman Empire and beyond.

———

Christ's resurrection
proved His divinity.

The resurrection of Christ has an important place in our faith for a variety of reasons:

1. Christ became the first person to return from death, never to die again. People like Lazarus, whom Jesus raised from the dead, later died again. Christ is "the firstfruits of those who have fallen asleep" (1 Cor. 15:20).
2. Christ's bodily resurrection is the example and guarantee of ours. Jesus told His disciples, "Because I live, you also will live" (John 14:19).
3. Christ's resurrection validated His ministry; everything He said and did was from the Father. People believed His message because God raised Him from the dead (Acts 17:31; 1 Cor. 15:21-26).
4. Christ's resurrection proved His divinity. As Paul put it, "Regarding his Son, who as to his human nature was a descendant of David, and who through the Spirit of holiness was declared with power to be the Son of God by his resurrection from the dead: Jesus Christ our Lord" (Rom. 1:3-4).
5. Christ's resurrection became the foundation stone of the Early Church. The apostles publicly proclaimed the gospel message to everyone on the streets of Jerusalem on the Day of Pentecost. This day became the birthday of the Church. The power point of their preaching centered on the resurrection of Christ (Acts 2:31-35).

Songwriter Robert Lowry summarized it best:

Up from the grave He arose,
With a mighty triumph o'er His foes.
He arose a Victor from the dark domain,
And He lives forever with His saints to reign.

The events surrounding Christ's crucifixion received full public attention. He died in public view, His death certified by a Roman soldier (Mark 15:44-45). Joseph and Nicodemus, leaders of the Jewish governing body, the Sanhedrin, buried Him in a public location (John 19:38-42). Soldiers guarded His grave (Matt. 27:65-66). But as Herbert

Booth Smith reminds, "Joseph's tomb wasn't a tomb at all—it was a room for a transient."[2]

The first public announcement of Christ's resurrection came not from His disciples, but from the soldier guards. They reported His empty grave to the chief priests, who then conspired with the soldiers to circulate a self-contradicting lie. They had the soldiers say the disciples had stolen His body while they slept (Matt. 28:11-15). How did they know what happened while they slept? Why would they admit to falling asleep while on duty if they knew they would be killed for shirking responsibility? No doubt a search was conducted, but no body ever surfaced. If a dead body existed, His Jewish and Roman enemies would have found it. Christ rose from the dead as He promised; His enemies knew it.

Jesus made at least 10 separate appearances to more than 518 people at a variety of locations. Some, like Thomas, did not want to believe the Resurrection but saw the miracle with their own eyes. None who saw it remained the same—their lives were revolutionized. Jesus' followers were so moved by this revelation that they changed their day of worship from Saturday to Sunday. The concept of "Resurrection power" became the energizing force for evangelization and the nurture of the Early Church (Phil. 3:10-11).

Using the Truth to Enrich Your Life

How would we live without batteries? Many things in my office run on batteries: computer, watch, tape recorder, telephone, clock, and the list goes on. They run down quickly in action toys but last for years in watches. Some are disposable, others rechargeable. Batteries provide an important source of energy for the many gadgets of life.

**If God the Father has the power
to raise Christ from the dead,
He has the power to help me
with my problem.**

When I think of the tremendous energy source it takes to operate the Christian Church worldwide and energize Christian individuals for daily life, I realize that great power is required. What is that energy source? The resurrection power of God. In Rom. 8 Paul discussed the idea of living the Christian life through the Spirit of God. In verse 11 He described the power source for that life: "And if the Spirit of him who raised Jesus from the dead is living in you, he who raised Christ from the dead will also give life to your mortal bodies through his Spirit, who lives in you."

Anytime I get discouraged over difficult situations and wonder how I'm going to make it through, I ask myself if my situation is more difficult or complicated than raising the dead. It never is, of course! If God the Father has the power to raise Christ from the dead, He has the power to help me with my problem.

Resurrection power differs from earthly energy sources in a number of ways.

1. It never runs down.
2. It doesn't need recharging.
3. It's always adequate.
4. It never comes up short when put to the test.
5. It doesn't pollute the environment.
6. Best of all, it's free for the asking.

So the next time you need extra divine help in your life, call on God for an extra measure of His resurrection power. He'll be more than happy to supply you with all you need.

Fast Takes

1. When Jesus died on the Cross, His disciples lost all hope and retreated in fear behind locked doors.
2. Christ's resurrection proved His divinity and became the foundation stone of the Early Church.
3. Resurrection power is the energizing force for the Church and our lives.

Prayer

May I realize, dear Father, the incredible Resurrection power You possess, not only to have brought Your Son back to life, but also to help me in daily life.

SALVATION

He who has the Holy Spirit in his heart and
the Scripture in his hands has all he needs.
—Alexander Maclaren

CHAPTER 6

GOD'S PRESENCE
WITHIN

THE WORK OF THE HOLY SPIRIT

Biblical Foundation

> *"I will give you a new heart and put a new spirit in you; I will remove from you your heart of stone and give you a heart of flesh"* (Ezek. 36:26).

> *"I will ask the Father, and he will give you another Counselor to be with you forever—the Spirit of truth. The world cannot accept him, because it neither sees him nor knows him. But you know him, for he lives with you and will be in you"* (John 14:16-17).

Jesus told His disciples about the Holy Spirit before His crucifixion. They had many questions about this special Person. Before He ascended back to heaven, He told them to wait and pray together until the Holy Spirit came to them. In the moment the Spirit filled them on the Day of Pentecost, they had most of their questions answered and received power in their lives, which helped them change their world.

The Truth Explained in Everyday Language

The disciples' hearts filled with sadness as they watched Jesus Christ ascend back to heaven from the Mount of Olives (Acts 1:1-10). Their sorrow turned into great joy, however, when God filled their hearts with the Holy Spirit on the Day of Pentecost (2:1-4). The coming of the Holy Spirit into believers' hearts signaled a new chapter in God's relationship with us. He brought us a new heart and a new spirit as Ezekiel promised (36:26); He came to live in us as Jesus promised (John 14:16-17). As Alfred, Lord Tennyson put it, "Closer is He than breathing, and nearer than hands and feet."[1]

A great deal of misunderstanding about the Holy Spirit developed across church history. His lack of physical form led some thinkers to incorrectly claim that He was not a person, but an impersonal force, the way God is often pictured in the movies. They presented the Holy Spirit as "it" rather than "Him." Others saw Him as an angel or a ministering spirit. Some saw Him subordinate to the Father and Son but not possessing deity, a sort of a low-class hired hand carrying out their orders.

The Holy Spirit is a person, like the Father and the Son, not an impersonal force.

The Bible gives us a clear picture of who the Holy Spirit is and what He does. The best information in the Bible comes from John 14—16.

The Holy Spirit is a person, like the Father and the Son, not an impersonal force. He has intelligence, will, and emotions. He is affected by our actions. In other words, we can grieve, resist, quench, and even blaspheme Him by the things we say, think, and do. He lives in relationship with us as a person. He speaks, commands, guides, illuminates, reveals, teaches, intercedes, and everything else true of a person. He is fully divine with the Father and the Son and is the third Member of the Trinity.

The Holy Spirit has been actively involved in our world since its beginning. His presence permeates the entire Old Testament. He worked with the other Members of the Trinity in creating the world and everything in it (Gen. 1:2). He inspired the writers of Scripture to record the message of God for us (2 Pet. 1:21). He worked with people, giving them special skills and abilities to accomplish His will (Exod. 31:3-5). He guided the leaders of Israel in the Old Testament (Num. 11:25; 1 Sam. 16:13). He spoke through the prophets (Joel 2:28-29).

The Holy Spirit actively participated in the earthly life and ministry of Jesus Christ. He placed the fetus of Jesus in Mary's body (Luke 1:35). He spoke through John the Baptist in preparing the way for Jesus (v. 15). He blessed Jesus through Simeon and Anna (2:25-38). He descended as a dove upon Jesus at His baptism (3:21-22). He prepared Jesus for His time of temptation (4:1). He empowered Jesus for His daily ministry (v. 14) and instructed Him in His teaching ministry (vv. 18-19). He performed miracles with Jesus (Matt. 12:28) and raised Him from the dead (Rom. 1:3-4).

The Holy Spirit brings the presence of God to our world today. He works particularly in restoring and maintaining our fellowship with the Father. He brings conviction to sinners, urges us to live righteous lives, and warns us of the coming Judgment (John 16:8). He gives us new birth and faith in God (3:3-5). Once we become a Christian, He lives in our heart and illuminates our mind to the things of God (14:16-17). He inspires our mind when we read the Bible and guides us to truth (16:13). He brings us the presence of the living Christ (vv. 15-16). He intercedes on our behalf to the Father (Rom. 8:26-27). He sanctifies our hearts by faith (vv. 1-17). He produces spiritual fruit in our lives (Gal. 5:22-23). He gives us gifts and abilities for ministry in His Church and to His world (Rom. 12, 1 Cor. 12, Eph. 4). He works through the Church to win new converts and glorify Christ. As D. L. Moody put it, the Holy Spirit is God at work in our world.[2]

Not only does the Holy Spirit bring God to us, but also He is our resident Friend, Counselor, Adviser, and Teacher.

The most significant work of the Holy Spirit is in bringing us God's presence and taking our thoughts and prayers back to the Father. God's presence does not remain outside us like light in a room. It is internalized, like a pacemaker placed inside the body. God lives within our hearts in a way unique to Christianity. Though He fills us, we never hold all of His presence. As one man prayed, "O Lord, we can't hold much, but we can overflow lots."[3]

Using the Truth to Enrich Your Life

Sue and I take a group of college students to the mission field each year to build buildings, minister, and witness for Christ. One of the most frustrating hindrances in the countries we visit is communication lag times. Often our work site is several miles from where we are staying, with team members at both locations. I need to get a message to students at the other location. Or the missionaries need to contact one another about building materials, food, or supplies. Inability to communicate frustrates us and hinders the work.

But our Brazil project had no communication problems. Missionaries carried cellular phones at all times. We were never out of touch with one another, regardless of the distance between us. I was amazed at our team's increased productivity and lower frustration level.

In a small way this illustrates the tremendous advantage we have because of the Holy Spirit living in our hearts. He brings the presence

of God as near as the missionaries' cellular phones brought them together. The Spirit is better than a cellular phone, however, because we
are never out of range of God's signal, we never pick up interference,
we don't have to worry about batteries running down, and we can't
misplace Him by accident.

Not only does the Holy Spirit bring God to us, but also He is our
resident Friend, Counselor, Adviser, and Teacher. Every area of our
Christian walk is made possible by the work of the Holy Spirit of God
in us. Everything we are and every success we have as Christians is a
result of His ministry to us. J. B. Phillips says the Holy Spirit is the living God "able and willing to enter human personality and change it."[4]

Fast Takes

1. The Holy Spirit is fully divine with the Father and the Son.
2. The Holy Spirit has been actively involved in our world since
   the beginning of time.
3. The Holy Spirit brings us the presence of God and takes our
   thoughts and prayers back to the Father.

Prayer

*Help me, Father, to realize I am never out of touch with You;
Your Holy Spirit lives within my heart.*

Just as I am! Thy love unknown
Hath broken ev'ry barrier down.
—Charlotte Elliott

CHAPTER 7

HEAVEN'S HOUND

PREVENIENT GRACE

Biblical Foundation

"*Restore me, and I will return, because you are the LORD my God. After I strayed, I repented; after I came to understand, I beat my breast. I was ashamed and humiliated because I bore the disgrace of my youth*" (Jer. 31:18-19).

"*We love because he first loved us*" (1 John 4:19).

Jesus said He came to seek and save the lost (Luke 19:10). They did not come looking for Him—*He* sought *them*. He went where people hurt and suffered so He could change their lives. His ministry clearly pictures God reaching out to find His lost children.

The Truth Explained in Everyday Language

We moved to Nashville when Brent was three years old. We finished unloading the moving truck late in the afternoon, just before dark. Furniture and boxes sat helter-skelter all over our newly rented house. All of a sudden, Sue couldn't find Brent. Our world stopped as we began to call out his name and look through the house and around the yard. All efforts failed to locate him. We spread our search to the neighborhood, Sue on foot and me in the car. My dad and the neighbors helped us. No doubt he had wandered off to explore his new surroundings. But he wasn't around the neighborhood either. Sue and I both panicked.

Just as I picked up the phone to call the police, Brent emerged from under the covered piano bench. He was so proud of himself. He had been playing hide-and-seek without telling us; he thought he had played well, because he hadn't given away his hiding place when we called his name repeatedly. I think he took five years off our lives that day!

Most people conceive of "finding God" or "getting religion" in terms of a game of hide-and-seek. God has hidden himself and dares us to find Him. If we are able to locate Him by going to church, talking to a religious friend, or reading a Bible, He will save us.

This analogy fails for two important reasons. First, we have neither the desire nor the means to initiate a search for God. Left to ourselves, we could not care less whether or not we know God. Second, God does not hide from us; He does everything within His power to reveal himself to us.

A better analogy pictures God taking the initiative, like a hound seeking us out. I remember as a child seeing our neighbor's hounds tirelessly sniffing for a squirrel or a raccoon. Once they picked up the trail, they followed the animal through field and forest until they treed it; then they stood at the base of the tree barking for their master to come.

**The very desire to find God
is a gift, as is the ability
and the will to repent.**

In that same way, God takes the initiative in searching for us. He reasons and pleads with us. He makes us an offer we ought not to refuse. He won't let us alone until we understand the terms and at least consider His offer of salvation. If we refuse, He keeps coming back, like a persistent lover, with fresh appeals to try and convince us to accept Him. Harry Ironside reminds us that God has been calling out to humanity since He called for Adam and Eve in the Garden of Eden.[1] We call God's persistence "prevenient grace."

The term "prevenient grace" literally means "grace that goes before." That is, it is all God graciously does before we get saved to bring us to a point of salvation. People all around us set bad examples in our sinful world. Sin has worked its way into life's systems; it's everywhere. But worst of all, original sin resides in our hearts, causing us to prefer self-interests. It predisposes us to act sinfully. Once we begin to sin, we head our lives in a direction away from God. Not only are we not doing what God wants us to do, but also we don't even *want* to do what God wants us to do. Even if we are aware of our sinful condition, we don't care. "So what?" we ask. Our lives spiral downward as we dig deeper into the habits and bondage of sin and farther from God.

Some people say our free wills were so damaged by the Fall that God's grace can't even enable us to choose Him. He must exercise His sovereign power to save from their sins whomever He chooses. The God who knows best gives salvation to some. We have no part in our salvation, not even a choice. This is an incorrect understanding of pre-destination. God does not decide our eternal destiny for us. He does not elect some to salvation and others to damnation. Such a view opposes the entire gospel message of a universal call. Our salvation involves working together with God; as He calls, we accept. He will not save us apart from our acceptance.

Some have tried to argue that we can use free will to choose to invite God into our lives anytime we like, the same way we choose to invite a friend to our house. Not so. Our free wills were so damaged by the Fall that our choices don't include God. That's the bad news. The good news is that God's prevenient grace overcomes that damage. The very desire we have to find God comes from His drawing influence on our lives. Jesus said, "No one can come to me unless the Father who sent me draws him" (John 6:44).

**God works quietly
behind the scenes
of our lives.**

We often speak of our salvation as a gift of God's grace, and it is. But the very desire to find God is also a gift, as is the ability and the will to repent. Therefore, the new birth itself is a further benefit of that grace. The ultimate gift of grace will be our reception into heaven to live with the Lord forever. All of this prompted Paul to say, "It is by grace you have been saved, through faith—and this not from yourselves, it is the gift of God—not by works, so that no one can boast" (Eph. 2:8-9). No room for pride here. As Charles Spurgeon put it, "The higher a man is in grace, the lower he will be in his own esteem."[2] From first to last, salvation is God's gracious gift to us.

Using the Truth to Enrich Your Life

How does God's prevenient grace find its way into our lives? Sometimes we hear it in our conscience warning us against a course of action. Sometimes it comes from a pastor or Christian friend or parent giving us sound advice. Sometimes the circumstances of life come at us in such a way that our thoughts turn to God. Sometimes our plans to do the wrong thing fall through, and our best efforts at having our own way won't work. Sometimes we are left dry and unsatisfied by the choices we have made in life.

Mere circumstances? I think not. These and a thousand other ways become God's means of making us stop and give our attention to Him. Usually He works quietly behind the scenes of our lives, but He works nonetheless. John Wesley called prevenient grace "preventing grace"—because it prevents us from getting too far away from God and His call to salvation.

Why is this doctrine so important? First, it reminds us of all God does to bring us to himself and establish or restore relationship. Second, it encourages us to continue to pray for our lost friends and loved ones. For some mysterious reason, God's prevenient grace works harder in the lives of people on our prayer lists. So pray on—God hasn't given up on our lost friends, and neither should we.

Fast Takes

1. Left to ourselves, we would have no desire for God or His ways.
2. God takes the initiative through His prevenient grace to seek us out.
3. Our ability to accept God's offer of salvation is His gift to us.

Prayer

Thank You, God, for coming to me when I had no desire to find You. Thank You for loving me and offering me Your salvation.

Many persons who appear to repent are like sailors who throw their goods overboard in a storm, and wish for them again in a calm.

—Mead

CHAPTER 8

ABOUT FACE!

REPENTANCE

Biblical Foundation

> "From that time on Jesus began to preach, 'Repent, for the kingdom of heaven is near'" (Matt. 4:17).

> "When the people heard this, they were cut to the heart and said to Peter and the other apostles, 'Brothers, what shall we do?' Peter replied, 'Repent and be baptized, every one of you, in the name of Jesus Christ for the forgiveness of your sins. And you will receive the gift of the Holy Spirit'" (Acts 2:37-38).

Jesus came to change people's lives. That change involved repentance. He called people to repent and turn to God as a first step in restoring their fellowship with Him. Jesus knew that a true change of heart involved more than determining to do better; it required a complete turnaround.

The Truth Explained in Everyday Language

One day in the sixth grade my friend Dan cooked up a plan to sneak away from school and get into mischief. Fortunately Mrs. Scnibley, our teacher, discovered his plan before he roped me into it too. Dan acted pretty cool until he got into deep trouble. Then he cried like a baby and spilled information like a leaky bucket. I think that day Dan confessed to Mrs. Scnibley everything he had done wrong in his entire life.

Dan's confession impressed me. I thought his repentance was

genuine—until the next day. Twenty-four hours later he was already devising his next scheme. What about yesterday's performance? Oh, he was truly sorry—sorry he had gotten caught, not sorry he did wrong. There's a big difference.

That big difference is central to understanding the repentance that pleases God. Repentance is a key for entering into right relationship with God and an essential feature of our salvation. We cannot become a Christian without it. Phineas F. Bresee reminded us, "Repentance means the forsaking of sin, the hating of what God hates, the loathing of our own iniquity, and the soul's deepest cry for mercy."[1] John the Baptist made repentance the focus of his ministry in preparing the way for Jesus Christ. "In those days John the Baptist came, preaching in the Desert of Judea and saying, 'Repent, for the kingdom of heaven is near'" (Matt. 3:1-2). Jesus himself emphasized repentance: "From that time on Jesus began to preach, 'Repent, for the kingdom of heaven is near'" (4:17).

For repentance to please God, four elements are necessary.

1. We must admit to ourselves that we have done wrong in God's sight. "If we claim to be without sin, we deceive ourselves and the truth is not in us" (1 John 1:8). Sinning—that is a very difficult thing for us to admit. Our pride gets in the way; we do not want to own our actions or attitudes when God brings them to our attention. We want to toss them like stray gloves into a lost-and-found box. The Holy Spirit faithfully convicts us of our sins, but we have to reach the point to admit them.

"To do it no more is the truest repentance."
—Martin Luther

2. We must be sorry—not sorry for getting caught, but rather sorry that we disobeyed God and broke His heart. Paul calls the first "worldly sorrow" and the second "godly sorrow." "Now I am happy, not because you were made sorry, but because your sorrow led you to repentance. For you became sorrowful as God intended and so were not harmed in any way by us. Godly sorrow brings repentance that leads to salvation and leaves no regret, but worldly sorrow brings death" (2 Cor. 7:9-10). Notice the different results of the two types of sorrow: salvation, death.

3. We confess our sins to God. Admitting them to ourselves and being sorry for them is good, but that's not enough. We must also confess them to God, the One we have wronged. Confession precedes God's forgiveness. "If we confess our sins, he is faithful and just and will forgive us our sins and purify us from all unrighteousness" (1 John 1:9).

4. We do an about-face like a soldier doing military exercises. That is, we turn our back on our sinful ways and quit them. We change our minds, which results in a change of behavior. As Martin Luther said, "To do it no more is the truest repentance."[2] Both the Old and New Testaments teach repentance. The Old Testament prophet Ezekiel said, "Therefore, O house of Israel, I will judge you, each one according to his ways, declares the Sovereign LORD. Repent! Turn away from all your offenses; then sin will not be your downfall" (18:30). In the New Testament, the apostle Peter said following Pentecost, "Repent, then, and turn to God, so that your sins may be wiped out, that times of refreshing may come from the Lord" (Acts 3:19).

This last step of turning around may also involve restitution, or going back and making our wrongs right. We can't always retrace our steps, but often we can. We must let God direct us to correct what is correctable. If we are sensitive, He will lead us in these matters. The Old Testament gave the Israelites clear formulas for restitution (Exod. 22:1-15). Zacchaeus modeled restitution well when he accepted Christ. He paid back with interest those he had defrauded (Luke 19:8-9). Restitution not only clears our own conscience but also gives clear witness of our faith to the world and gives God an opportunity to work in the hearts of others.

Genuine repentance, then, involves getting honest with yourself and with God, being truly sorry for your ways, confessing your condition to God, and changing your mind and behavior about sinful actions and attitudes. When those elements are all present, we are in a position for God to help us.

Using the Truth to Enrich Your Life

I will always remember the first time I openly confronted Brent with his wrongdoing. One day when he was two years old, he was playing in the living room by himself. From the dining room I watched him disobey a family rule—"Don't climb on the coffee table." After he finished his little escapade in disobedience and climbed down, I walked into the living room. I asked him if he had been climbing on the coffee table. He said he hadn't. I confronted him with his response. He again flatly denied any wrongdoing. I finally told him what I had seen from the dining room. He became totally silent for several seconds with the strangest look of guilt in his eyes.

I said, "Admit to Dad that you did it."

"No!" he declared.

We each repeated our last statements. I waited as our wills clashed. Finally he broke down and cried out, "OK—I did it." I quickly forgave him, and we hugged like two bears.

It is usually as hard for adults to admit to themselves and God that they have sinned as it was for Brent to admit his wrongdoing to me. But admission is necessary. Until we own it, we can't get past it. Several of my friends are living in bondage to their actions and attitudes, but they are also living in denial. God can never free them until they acknowledge their problem.

———

God is faithful—
He will grant us the power
to stay true to our decision to serve Him.

Beyond admission, we have to quit the sinning business—cold turkey. Habits, needs, desires, instincts, and drives are all strong and get a hold on our lives. We'll be tempted to return to our old ways. But God is faithful—He will grant us the power to stay true to our decision to serve Him. His grace brings us to a point of repentance, and it can keep us from returning to our old ways.

Fast Takes

1. Jesus said repentance is necessary for salvation.
2. Repentance is being sorry enough to quit sinning.
3. Repentance involves getting honest with yourself and with God, being truly sorry for your ways, confessing your condition to God, and changing your mind and behavior about sinful actions and attitudes.

Prayer

Help me to be open and honest with myself before You, O God, so I can see my thoughts and behavior as You see them.

*The object of our faith must be Christ. Not
faith in ritual, not faith in sacrifices, not faith
in morals, not faith in yourself—not faith in
anything but Christ!*

—Billy Graham

CHAPTER 9

SIMPLY TRUSTING

SAVING FAITH

Biblical Foundation

*"These are written that you may believe that Jesus is the
Christ, the Son of God, and that by believing you may have life in
his name" (John 20:31).*

*"I am not ashamed of the gospel, because it is the power of God
for the salvation of everyone who believes: first for the Jew, then for
the Gentile. For in the gospel a righteousness from God is revealed,
a righteousness that is by faith from first to last, just as it is written: 'The righteous will live by faith'" (Rom. 1:16-17).*

Jesus spoke often in His ministry about believing in Him. In fact,
nearly 50 verses can be found in the Gospel of John alone on believing
in Jesus. What did He mean? He meant simply trusting in Him alone
for our salvation.

The Truth Explained in Everyday Language

When Martin Luther read Rom. 1:16-17 in his devotional time, he
realized simple faith in Christ alone is all that is required for right
standing with God. It led to his famous Reformation position of "salvation by grace through faith alone"—not religious rituals, not religious pilgrimages, not giving money to the church, not teaching a religious class, not serving on church governing bodies, not crawling on

one's knees before a religious shrine. Nothing but believing in Jesus alone for salvation will lead to salvation. Billy Graham observed, "It's so easy to receive Christ that millions stumble over its sheer simplicity."[1]

What is involved in simply trusting in Jesus Christ?

1. We throw away our confidence in trying to please God any other way. It's like throwing away a worn, dirty article of clothing. Human nature instinctively searches for ways to earn God's favor. Through one good deed or another we hope to put ourselves in a position of winning God's approval, like a child trying to please a parent. We must realize that the problem of sin is too big for us; we cannot earn favor with God. With this awareness, we empty our hands of everything intended for God. Inability to please Him is highlighted in Pss. 14:1-3; 53:1-3; Eccles. 7:20; and Rom. 3:10-18.

———

Our entire hope of salvation and heaven grows out of our simple trust in Jesus Christ alone for our salvation.

2. We commit ourselves voluntarily to the Jesus Christ portrayed throughout the New Testament. We come empty-handed as we bow before Him in submission, a rebel holding up the white flag of surrender. Our ways haven't worked. So we give them all up and offer ourselves to Christ. As a well-known hymn says, "I surrender all" (J. W. Van DeVenter). Jesus is someone to whom we owe more than a gold-plated figurine; we own Him our lives.

3. We embrace Christ as God's plan for our lives and the only hope of our salvation. The vacant area in our heart created by throwing away our confidence in every other way and by self-surrender fills with the personal presence of Christ. This presence comes to us through the power of the Holy Spirit, who lives within us.

Saving faith is not a feeling; it is an intellectual, psychological, emotional, and spiritual resolve to believe and live the truth of the gospel message as presented in the New Testament. When I think of simply trusting, I picture the way Brent trusted me to catch him when he jumped into the swimming pool as a small child. He believed me enough to put his life in my hands. That's what we do when we resolve to follow Christ. Feelings come and feelings go, but a resolve to follow Christ is a commitment that goes beyond daily circumstances and feelings. We build all of life around this trust in God. Raymond Lindquist sees it as walking over a bridge you know will hold you up.[2]

The best and worst examples of saving faith are found in the Old Testament. The best example features Abraham. His story appears originally in Gen. 12—25. His faith is highlighted in Rom. 4. Paul points out that Abraham found favor with God by his faith alone. "What does the Scripture say? 'Abraham believed God, and it was credited to him as righteousness'" (Rom. 4:3, cf. 22; Gen. 15:6). The worst example of salvation faith features the Exodus generation of Israelites (Exod. 15—40). God delivered them from Egypt, supplied their every need in the desert, and watched over them like a mother hen. They responded to His concern with disrespect, contempt, and lack of faith.

More than just a onetime act of believing, salvation faith becomes a permanent attitude of daily life. As Paul put it, "So then, just as you received Christ Jesus as Lord, continue to live in him, rooted and built up in him, strengthened in the faith as you were taught, and overflowing with thankfulness" (Col. 2:6-7). This faith becomes a liberating law of life that frees us from our old way of life. "Therefore, there is now no condemnation for those who are in Christ Jesus, because through Christ Jesus the law of the Spirit of life set me free from the law of sin and death" (Rom. 8:1-2). Our entire hope of salvation and heaven grows out of our simple trust in Jesus Christ alone for our salvation. As G. Campbell Morgan said, "I believe the promises of God enough to venture an eternity on them."[3]

Using the Truth to Enrich Your Life

My upper-division theology students hate my exams. They accuse me of working late into the night to think up trick questions. They look forward to taking the final exam and being done with my "twisted tests" forever. They often ask if we're going to be required to take a test to get into heaven. They look surprised when I tell them yes. Then I go on to explain.

———

**We call it "childlike faith"
because it's simple enough
for even a child
to understand and accept.**

The entrance exam to heaven has only one essay question on it. The question is "On what or in whom are you trusting for your salvation?" Let me drop you an exam hint: don't list all the church services you attended, the money you gave to the church or charity, the hours you invested in helping others, the number of times you read your Bible entirely through in a year, or the hours you clocked in prayer. Unlike my essay test questions, this one has a simple answer: we base our salvation on simply trusting in Jesus Christ alone.

How does this relate to daily life on earth? In those quiet times when the haunting questions of life come creeping in, like "What is going to happen after I die?" and "What do I need to be doing to get ready to meet my Maker?" rest assured that all you need to do is simply believe in Jesus Christ. Put all your confidence in Him; rest all your doubts, misgivings, and misunderstandings in Him; find your highest joy and greatest fulfillment in Him. We call it "childlike faith" because it's simple enough for even a child to understand and accept. But it's effective enough to save our soul for eternity.

Fast Takes

1. Salvation by grace through faith means we simply trust in Christ alone for our salvation.
2. Saving faith is not a feeling; it is a spiritual resolve to believe and live by the truth of the gospel message.
3. Saving faith becomes a permanent attitude for daily life.

Prayer

Thank You, God, for taking all the guesswork out of salvation and giving me saving faith.

*I think that if God forgives us we must forgive
ourselves. Otherwise it is almost like setting
up ourselves as a higher tribunal than Him.*
—C. S. Lewis

CHAPTER 10

NOT GUILTY

JUSTIFICATION

Biblical Foundation

*"Since we have been justified through faith, we have peace
with God through our Lord Jesus Christ, through whom we have
gained access by faith into this grace in which we now stand. And
we rejoice in the hope of the glory of God"* (Rom. 5:1-2).

*"Just as the result of one trespass was condemnation for all
men, so also the result of one act of righteousness was justification
that brings life for all men"* (Rom. 5:18).

Jesus spoke often about right standing with God. He said a path
needed to be cleared between the Father and us. He came to do just
that. A lot of wonderful things happen when we become Christians.
The first is that we are made right in God's sight because of what
Christ did on the Cross for us.

The Truth Explained in Everyday Language

At the end of each school year at the university where I teach, we
have an awards chapel in which the faculty and administration present certain students with awards. These fit into two basic categories.
Some are earned by scoring the highest grade on a particular test,
writing the best newspaper article, or accumulating the most points in
a sport. These awards resemble receiving a wage that students worked
hard to get. Other awards are given because of the recipients' financial
need. Such scholarship grants enable students to return to school next

year to continue their studies. They resemble unearned gifts that are given out of the kindness of someone's heart.

These two types of awards illustrate the different ways people believe they are justified in God's sight. We know we must please God or reach some standard in order to get to heaven. But how do we do it? Surveys indicate that most people think we earn our way to God through good works. We show kindness to everyone around us every day. We go to church, read our Bible, and pray. We repay evil with good. We smile, sing, and say encouraging words every chance we get. Then, when we die, God places all our good deeds on one side of His balance scales and our bad deeds on the other side. If our good deeds outweigh our bad, we get into heaven.

So help from God comes on the basis of need, not good performance.

This idea makes God's system of justice like a soft drink machine. We place our good deeds, like pocket change, into the machine. God is obligated to give us a ticket into heaven because our actions have earned it. We simply take possession of what He owes us. This may be the most popular notion, but it is not the biblical one.

The Bible presents a picture more in keeping with the second type of award we give at school. Our good deeds earn us no favor with God. He says our acts of righteousness are like filthy rags when it comes to purchasing His favor (Isa. 64:6). Ever tried to pay your bill at the department store with a sack of grease rags? Don't try it—they don't have any purchasing power. So help from God comes on the basis of need, not good performance. Our acceptance by God is an unearned gift from the kindness of His heart. It comes from His unbounded generosity.

Paul says in Rom. 5:1 that we have been justified in God's sight. Does that mean that God *declares* us righteous or that He *makes* us righteous? In other words, does He view us through Christ's sacrifice on the Cross and see us better than we really are? Or does He transform our hearts and lives so we can please Him? People have argued this point both ways for many years. The good news is that both are true.

Christ's sacrificial death on the Cross enables the Father to see us through eyes of grace and mercy. God *declares* us free from the guilt and penalty of our past sins and gives us a new start. This is the spiritual life Christ brings us. With sins forgiven, God accepts us as justified in His sight. We can break apart the word justification and define

it: "just as if I'd never sinned." As Paul put it, "There is now no condemnation for those who are in Christ Jesus" (Rom. 8:1).

But God does not stop there. He does not see us as righteous
while we continue to sin every day. Such a view pictures God as a
blind grandparent who thinks his grandchildren are well behaved
when in fact they're tearing the house apart. No. God's work of justification also *makes* us righteous. When He forgives us of our sins, He
empowers us by His grace to do what is right. We are righteous, not
only because we have been declared righteous, but also because we
now do right things. John Wesley reminds us, "Least of all does justification imply, that God is deceived in those whom he justifies; that he
thinks them to be what, in fact, they are not; that he accounts them to
be otherwise than they are. . . . The plain scriptural notion of justification is pardon, the forgiveness of sins."[1]

Keep the following ideas in mind as you think about justification.

1. We are justified in God's sight when we simply trust in Christ
   as our personal Savior. We have saving faith in Him.
2. Justification is both an act of God and a state in which we live
   as we continue to trust in Christ on a daily basis. Thus, we can
   say, "I have been justified" (act), and "I am being justified daily" (state). We can add to that, "I will be justified" when I
   stand before God on Judgment Day and hear Him declare my
   justification for all eternity.
3. Justification takes something away and gives something. Our
   sinful record is destroyed. God hits the delete button on His
   computer, and the record is gone forever. He gives us acceptance by adding our names to His list of children.
4. The act of God's justification happens in a moment. We do not
   gradually grow into it. In the blink of an eye, God forgives us
   of all our sins, removes our guilt, releases us from sin's penalty,
   declares us righteous, and makes us new creatures so we can
   begin to live right in His sight. That's quite a sweeping move!
5. God both forgives and forgets our sins. The Bible often speaks
   of His forgiveness (Matt. 26:28; Luke 24:47; Acts 2:38). Our sins
   would not really be taken away from us if He continued to remember the ways we had disobeyed Him and held them over
   our head the way a blackmailer does. "As far as the east is from
   the west, so far has he removed our transgressions from us"
   (Ps. 103:12). God expects us to do the same in forgiving ourselves. C. S. Lewis has it right—if God forgives and forgets, so
   must we.

Using the Truth to Enrich Your Life

I remember a particular time when as a child I disobeyed my

mother. I have long since forgotten what I did wrong. There were so many things, it's hard to keep them sorted out! My infraction is not the object of this story; her discipline is. She announced that my punishment would be pulling weeds in the garden. I hated pulling weeds. The sun was hot, and the garden was big enough to feed an army. After announcing my punishment, she said, "Let's get started." She went with me to the garden and worked right beside me until the job was done.

Our justification is yet another product of His great grace toward us.

That's a little like what God did in providing for our salvation. He announced our condemnation for disobedience against Him. Then He paid the price of our salvation so He could justify us in His sight. In my illustration my mother helped me, but I still had to work too. When it came to our salvation, God did it all. All we need to do is accept it and say, "Thank You." It's not automatic, like direct deposit at the bank—I must accept this gift of salvation.

We must always remember that we can never earn our salvation by the good deeds we perform. Such deeds should follow our justification, however, as the fruit of a changed heart. But we must never think of good fruit as earned favor with God. Our justification is yet another product of His great grace toward us.

Fast Takes

1. Favor with God is not earned by doing good deeds.
2. Justification in God's sight means He both *declares* us righteous and *makes* us righteous.
3. Justification with God comes through simply trusting Christ.

Prayer

I know I can never earn Your favor, dear God. Help me to accept Your gift of justification as I learn to understand it better.

To be born anew is to undergo such a radical change that it is like a new birth; the whole process is not a human achievement, because it comes from the grace and power of God.
—William Barclay

CHAPTER II

A NEW START

REGENERATION

Biblical Foundation

> "Now there was a man of the Pharisees named Nicodemus, a member of the Jewish ruling council. He came to Jesus at night and said, 'Rabbi, we know you are a teacher who has come from God. For no one could perform the miraculous signs you are doing if God were not with him.' In reply Jesus declared, 'I tell you the truth, no one can see the kingdom of God unless he is born again'" (John 3:1-3).

> "If anyone is in Christ, he is a new creation; the old has gone, the new has come!" (2 Cor. 5:17).

Jesus selected 12 ordinary men to be His disciples. He chose fishermen, tax collectors, and other blue-collar workers. Yet, after the gospel changed their lives, they rocked the Jewish and Roman worlds of their day. Nothing explains their transformation but the regenerating power of God working in them.

The Truth Explained in Everyday Language

Nicodemus served in the Sanhedrin, the prestigious ruling body of Israel's religion. He visited with Jesus at night, perhaps to have a few undisturbed moments from the busy schedule, or perhaps to talk with Jesus without public attention. Jesus introduced him to a revolutionary concept—new birth. Many of us have heard it all our lives, so it doesn't sound so revolutionary to us. But it surely went over Nicodemus's head, like trying to explain electricity to the apostle Peter. What on earth was Jesus talking about?

Jesus couched a spiritual concept in figurative language. He said our new life in Him differs so radically from our old sinful life that the transformation can best be described as rebirth. Our first birth gives us physical life, our second spiritual life. John Wesley explains the need for such a rebirth: "This, then, is the foundation of the new birth,—the entire corruption of our nature. Hence it is, that, being born in sin, we must be 'born again.' Hence every one that is born of a woman must be born of the Spirit of God."[1]

Regeneration, or the new birth, happens the moment a person repents and has faith in Jesus Christ.

Regeneration, or the new birth, happens the moment a person repents and has faith in Jesus Christ. God justifies us first, the subject of our last chapter. He forgives our sins. Then He grants us new spiritual life. Sin broke our relationship with God; new birth restores it. Just as religious observance and good works cannot justify us with God, neither can they give us spiritual life. Such religious performance only mocks our sad cry for fulfillment and leaves us spiritually dead and searching for something more, like a beggar looking for food in a garbage dumpster.

God the Holy Spirit performs this miraculous transformation in the heart of the new believer. Paul said, "You show that you are a letter from Christ, the result of our ministry, written not with ink but with the Spirit of the living God, not on tablets of stone but on tablets of human hearts" (2 Cor. 3:3). It comes by simply believing in Christ for eternal salvation: "Everyone who believes that Jesus is the Christ is born of God" (1 John 5:1). Paul describes this dramatic change in believers as "a new creation; the old has gone, the new has come!" (2 Cor. 5:17). John Wesley comments, "The life-transformation that comes when we are joined to Christ by faith is nothing short of a new creation. . . . All things are now viewed through the love of Christ."[2]

With our sins forgiven and a clean slate with God, regeneration restores us to our condition prior to our first sin. God tears all of the sin-stained pages out of our book. Things return to the way God intended them when He created us. With the power of sin broken in our lives, we can now live daily as He wants us to live. We now have an internal desire to serve God and do right.

We cannot grow into this experience in the way a child grows up.

It does not simply happen through natural development or maturity. It is neither turning over a new leaf nor making a New Year's resolution. It involves more than a resolve to do better. Our minds do not simply control our will and body. Neither education nor baptism secure it. We do not make a casual nod toward God to receive it. The new birth is the miraculous gift of God given when we place our faith and confidence in Jesus Christ.

Along with becoming a child of God, we are adopted into His family. Like adopted children, wanted and loved very much by their new parents, God loves us right into His family. We receive all of the spiritual benefits of relationship with Him. Paul described it by saying, "In love he predestined us to be adopted as his sons through Jesus Christ, in accordance with his pleasure and will—to the praise of his glorious grace, which he has freely given us in the One he loves" (Eph. 1:4-6). We now have the confidence of a child in the embrace of a parent. We know our Big Brother Jesus Christ supports us, and we know our new relationship will last eternally. As my elementary Sunday School teacher Mrs. St. John used to say, "We begin to really live only when we are born again."

Using the Truth to Enrich Your Life

People desperately long for a chance to start over. Signs all around us proclaim it. People constantly change jobs, move, buy new houses and new cars, get divorces, and remarry. Why? Because they want a new start. Maybe this new job or new town or new house or new car or new mate will give the opportunity to correct mistakes and get it right this time. The advertising industry and rampant consumerism fuel this need.

We can receive
a new start from God.

Advertising executives and product designers know that most people search for something offering a fresh start. So they promise that their service or product will do just that. Simply purchase their car or grooming product or electronic device, and you'll get a new lease on life. Self-help books fill bookstore shelves with promises of a new start or a new lease.

It all sounds so good, but it doesn't work. That's why people keep looking and buying and experimenting with new products or new jobs. Why? Because troubles follow people to their new setting. Their profession, location, or mate isn't the problem. Their problem lives within. True, they need to start over, but the start must begin internally. The advertising industry doesn't advertise products or services that work within. They only slap salve on symptoms. So the search continues for a chance to start over.

The good news is that we can receive a new start from God. When people with secular backgrounds hear this, they often think it sounds too good to be possible. Yet those of us who have experienced it almost take it for granted. Think about it for a minute. What if we could tell people that God can forgive their past, wipe their slate clean, and give them a fresh start? What if we could tell them that God can change them so they can do better next time? We can! That's the life-changing power of God.

Fast Takes

1. Jesus told Nicodemus he needed to be born again.
2. God grants new birth, or regeneration, when we put our faith in Christ.
3. Regeneration restores us to the way we were before we sinned.
4. Regeneration adopts us into the family of God.

Prayer

In a world of sin and defeat, thank You, Father, for a new start with a new life.

I felt my heart strangely warmed. I felt I did trust in Christ, Christ alone for my salvation; and an assurance was given me that He had taken away my sins, even mine, and saved me from the law of sin and death.

—John Wesley

CHAPTER 12

GOD'S AFFIRMING VOICE

WITNESS OF THE SPIRIT

Biblical Foundation

"You did not receive a spirit that makes you a slave again to fear, but you received the Spirit of sonship. And by him we cry, 'Abba, Father.' The Spirit himself testifies with our spirit that we are God's children" (Rom. 8:15-16).

"You also were included in Christ when you heard the word of truth, the gospel of your salvation. Having believed, you were marked in him with a seal, the promised Holy Spirit, who is a deposit guaranteeing our inheritance until the redemption of those who are God's possession—to the praise of his glory" (Eph. 1:13-14).

At the Last Supper Jesus promised His disciples He would send them another Comforter, to be with them forever. He spoke, of course, of the Holy Spirit. He said the Spirit would live in their hearts and bring them messages from God. These messages often remind us of God's love and His assurance of salvation.

The Truth Explained in Everyday Language

God never leaves us guessing. He accepts our repentant heart, forgives us of our sins, justifies us in His sight, grants us new birth, and adopts us into His family. Then He assures us the work is done. He welcomes us with a personal message from His heart. It's like getting a phone call from the bank president when we open a new checking account. No, we don't hear an audible voice, but He gives assurance to our conscious mind. John Wesley wrote in a 1725 letter to his mother that he was "persuaded we may know for certain if we are now in a state of salvation."[1] A friend once described God's assurance as "rock and roll"—"I'm on the Rock down here and the roll up there."

Words fail to describe the sense of God's presence in our hearts, but it is unlike any other experience in life.

This is more than an emotional release, though people sometimes laugh, cry, or show other emotional responses. It is more than wishful thinking; we cannot duplicate the wonderful sense of God's presence through positive thinking or meditation. It's more than a friend's suggestion; God's assurance goes much deeper than that. Words fail to describe the sense of God's presence in our hearts, but it is unlike any other experience in life. Some describe it as peace or release. Others describe a clean feeling inside. Still others say it feels like a ton of bricks having been lifted from their shoulders. Whatever the expression or the image, we somehow know our sins are forgiven and we are God's children. The old-timers used to describe the mystery by saying, "It's better felt than 'telt.'"

Not only does God give us a direct witness of His Spirit, but also He grants us an indirect witness as well. This comes in a variety of ways. People watch our lives and see something different about us. We begin to give evidence that God is working in us. We treat folks differently. We smile more. Our disposition changes for the better. We have more patience. These and a hundred other clues testify to our new relationship with God. Another evidence of the indirect witness comes in the mirror. We watch ourselves every day and see a big difference. Our new lifestyle is as much a mystery to us as it is to everyone else. The change surprises even us.

Spiritual fruit begins to grow. Paul called it "the fruit of the Spirit" in Gal. 5:22-23: "The fruit of the Spirit is love, joy, peace, patience, kindness, goodness, faithfulness, gentleness and self-control. Against such things there is no law." We can't use these verses as a ruler with which to unchristianize people when we don't think they're measuring up. We don't know how far God has already brought them. He may be doing more in their lives than any of us realize. Maybe we should have known them before the Lord started working on them! Our concern should be with ourselves. We look for growth and development as God works with us. It's like what a friend of mine recently said: "Anybody knows a piece of good fruit, don't they?" We watch for the good fruit to grow.

God gives every believer the witness of the Spirit. The Holy Spirit living and working in our lives reminds me of a down payment on a house you want to purchase. People house-shop all the time. It doesn't cost anything to look. However, when they find a house they think they would truly like to purchase, they give the seller a check to hold while the loan papers clear. This down payment check means the buyers are serious about the transaction. It's more than wishful thinking—money sits on the table.

The same is true with God's gift of the Holy Spirit to our hearts. His presence in our lives is like a down payment check. He is serious about taking us to heaven when we die. The Holy Spirit becomes our Guarantee that in God's mind, it's a done deal.

Using the Truth to Enrich Your Life

People desperately long to know if anything is "for sure" anymore. Our society has lost sight of certainty about anything. It is floating on a sea of relativism, subjectivism, and situationism. In our search to be tolerant of all positions, to give every view an equal standing, and to be politically correct in our conversation, we have created a society that is sure of nothing.

**We can know that God
accepts our repentant heart,
forgives us of our sins,
justifies us in His sight,
grants us new birth, and
adopts us into the family of God.**

We have raised an entire generation on uncertainty. But uncertainty is not a solid foundation on which to build life. From deep within the human heart comes a cry to know certainty, to build on bedrock. People are tired of being told that everything in life is relative. They have tried to build their lives on uncertainty, and it's not solid enough to support the weight of daily living. And so they search on, looking for something solid.

We can know that God accepts our repentant heart, forgives us of our sins, justifies us in His sight, grants us new birth, and adopts us into the family of God. People long for a solid foundation to build their lives on. They want to know something for sure. This is it!

So many things in our world are constantly changing—the weather patterns, the news, the technology, our circumstances in life, even our image in the mirror changes. Everything changes, that is, except for God and His promises to us. They remain constant with the changes of circumstances and time. He promised to take us to heaven to be with Him forever, and He gave us His Spirit to confirm it. We can take that to the bank!

Fast Takes

1. When we accept Christ as our Savior, God speaks to our heart and tells us we are His child. This is the direct witness of the Spirit.
2. The indirect witness comes from people looking at our lives, and our looking in the mirror to see a difference in our actions and attitudes.
3. The witness of the Spirit is God's down payment, guaranteeing us a place in heaven.

Prayer

In a world of uncertainty, help me to build my life on the solid foundation of Your assurance, dear God.

Holiness consists in doing the will of God with a smile.

—Mother Teresa

CHAPTER 13

HOLY AND HIS

ENTIRE SANCTIFICATION

Biblical Foundation

> *"May God himself, the God of peace, sanctify you through and through. May your whole spirit, soul and body be kept blameless at the coming of our Lord Jesus Christ. The one who calls you is faithful and he will do it" (1 Thess. 5:23-24).*

> *"I urge you, brothers, in view of God's mercy, to offer your bodies as living sacrifices, holy and pleasing to God—this is your spiritual act of worship. Do not conform any longer to the pattern of this world, but be transformed by the renewing of your mind. Then you will be able to test and approve what God's will is—his good, pleasing and perfect will" (Rom. 12:1-2).*

Jesus spoke often about being totally sold out to God. He said becoming a Christian is like selling all you have and taking the money to buy a valuable pearl. Or it's like taking all your money to buy a piece of property that has buried treasure on it. Jesus told the rich young ruler that he needed to sell his possessions and follow Him. Jesus did not oppose owning possessions, but He was opposed to them becoming our gods. Being the person God wants us to be requires a total sell-out.

The Truth Explained in Everyday Language

The Christian journey begins the moment we ask Christ into our lives. It continues until we go to be with the Lord forever. As we grow and develop in our faith, God opens new doors of commitment through which we walk. Entire sanctification is one of those new doors.

The Bible often speaks of sanctification, which basically means the total, lifelong process of becoming holy. Because the process begins with the new birth, we call the spiritual growth immediately following regeneration "initial sanctification." That is, we begin walking God's way. The fruit of the Spirit in our lives becomes evidence that a change has taken place.

This process of spiritual growth may continue for months or even years before we sense a need for something more in our Christian journey. The common experience of saints down through the ages has been an awareness of a remaining hindrance to further spiritual progress. No outward sin—just an uncertain gnawing for something more. This awareness usually takes the form of an internal battle with the self, such as Paul described in Gal. 5:16-26. In summary he said, "The sinful nature desires what is contrary to the Spirit, and the Spirit what is contrary to the sinful nature. They are in conflict with each other, so that you do not do what you want" (v. 17).

Once we pinpoint the self-centeredness, we realize it must be replaced with Christ-centeredness.

The battle may be self-centeredness in the form of self-seeking, self-assertion, self-indulgence, self-sufficiency, or self-will—all as a preference over God or others. It's not that we don't wish to please God—we do. Our problem involves wanting the best of both worlds: having what God wants *and* what we want at the same time. We realize we cannot have it both ways. We discussed the concept of self-centeredness in the chapter on original sin in the previous volume of *Coffee Shop Theology*. We have been plagued with this problem since the Fall in the Garden of Eden.

Once we pinpoint the self-centeredness, we realize it must be replaced with Christ-centeredness. We confess our need to God and surrender ourselves completely to His will. The old-timers called it "dying out to self." They did not mean self-extinction or psychological suicide; rather, they meant self-preference replaced with God-preference. After full surrender comes faith in God to change us. We trust God to accept our consecration and fill us completely with His Holy Spirit. The Spirit entered our life when we accepted Christ; now we are inviting Him to take charge of our control center.

Entire sanctification is God's gift. We do not earn or deserve it any more than we earned or deserved regeneration. We consecrate; God sanctifies. So the two experiences of grace are similar in that we ask in faith, and God grants us His gift. The two differ in a number of important ways, however. In regeneration we come to God as a rebel; in entire sanctification we come as a child of God seeking a deeper commitment. In regeneration we repent of wrongdoing; in entire sanctification we consecrate our wills and lives for all God wants to do with us. In regeneration we come with the guilt of a sinful lifestyle; in entire sanctification we come with the frustration and hindrance of a sin principle that causes us to prefer self.

The difference between our spiritual progress before and after entire sanctification centers on the removal of the hindrance of self-sovereignty.

Biblical terminology indicates that entire sanctification happens in a moment of time. Symbols include a baptism (Acts 1:5), a sealing (2 Cor. 1:22), a crucifixion (Rom. 6:6), and a circumcision (Col. 2:11). None of these symbols suggest a long process. Verb usage in the original language also indicates an immediate experience. For example, the Greek aorist tense suggests an event occurring at a moment in time. Nevertheless, the immediate experience must give way to a lifetime of growth in grace. The difference between our spiritual progress before and after entire sanctification centers on the removal of the hindrance of self-sovereignty. We now have a new openness to God's direction in our lives.

Just prior to Jesus' ascension back to heaven from the Mount of Olives, He told His disciples, "You will receive power when the Holy Spirit comes on you; and you will be my witnesses in Jerusalem, and in all Judea and Samaria, and to the ends of the earth" (Acts 1:8). The apostle Peter summarized the lasting results of entire sanctification when he spoke to the Jerusalem Council, comparing the events at Cornelius's house with Pentecost. He said, "God, who knows the heart, showed that he accepted them by giving the Holy Spirit to them, just as he did to us. He made no distinction between us and them, for he purified their hearts by faith" (15:8-9). Together these two passages remind us that the lasting results of entire sanctification are power and purity.

Some refer to entire sanctification as "Christian perfection." Many people don't like that term because they misunderstand it to mean the entirely sanctified believe they are perfect. John Wesley also did not like the term for that reason. He continued to use it, however, because it's biblical. Jesus said, "Be perfect, therefore, as your heavenly Father is perfect" (Matt. 5:48). Since we are still human and continue to make mistakes and fall short of a perfect standard of conduct, what kind of "perfect" are we talking about? We mean perfect in motive and desire to please God. Our actions are not flawless, but our intentions are pure. We want to please God more than anything else in the world. Thus, as Mother Teresa saw it, it is "doing the will of God with a smile." Years of maturity and growth will bring our performance more into line with the desires of our heart. God's Spirit continues to work with us to complete that process.

Using the Truth to Enrich Your Life

Recently Sue and I visited our friends Chip and Dana in southern California. Dana showed us to the guest bedroom and said, "Make yourselves at home." Now, she didn't really mean it. She meant we had their permission to hang our clothes in the closet and spread our personal items around the bedroom. She also meant we could use the iron or eat food from the kitchen. But that's about it. When I'm at our home, I can move the furniture, hang up new pictures, and even knock out a wall if I want to enlarge a room. I doubt if our friends would have appreciated our rearranging their living room furniture or conducting a garage sale of their possessions.

Something like our California visit exists in our relationship with God. We invite Him into our lives when we become a Christian. He is a guest in our hearts. He has control of us—within the limits we set. Our lives reflect His presence in ways people can see. In time, however, we begin to sense some resistance on our part to His additional requests for more control. We liked it just fine when His presence brought us peace and joy. Now He seems to be going a little too far by asking more than we care to give, like an Internal Revenue Service agent going through our financial records and wanting more tax money.

God wants full control of our entire being. It comes down to a question of who is going to call the shots in life—us or God. If we retain control, we hinder further spiritual growth; the relationship suffers. If we give Him control, we fear He might ask us to do something we don't want to do, like becoming a missionary to Bugville or shaving our head. Then we wouldn't be happy. Nonsense. That is Satan's lie. God's full control is the most liberating way to live. It is a blessed abandonment of self-interest. God always has our best interest in mind, and He seeks to do more in us than we ever dreamed possible. That's what makes entire sanctification the greatest adventure in our spiritual journey. Giving God everything pays dividends for all eternity.

Fast Takes

1. Entire sanctification is the gift of God that replaces our self-centeredness with Christ-centeredness.

2. It is received by faith in a moment of time, the same way we receive regeneration.
3. It is like stepping through a door into a room of growth, which continues for the rest of our lives.

Prayer

Praise You, Lord, for the promise of full salvation that not only forgives my sins but deals with my self-centeredness as well. Help me to grow in Christlikeness the rest of my days on earth.

Growth is the only evidence of life.
—John Henry Newman

CHAPTER 14

BECOMING MORE CHRISTLIKE

GROWTH IN GRACE

Biblical Foundation

"Like newborn babies, crave pure spiritual milk, so that by it you may grow up in your salvation" (1 Pet. 2:2).

"Grow in the grace and knowledge of our Lord and Savior Jesus Christ. To him be glory both now and forever! Amen" (2 Pet. 3:18).

Jesus compared the Christian life to physical life. The birth, growth, and development of a baby into a mature adult parallels the spiritual pilgrimage of a person who becomes a Christian. Most of the Bible's message aims to help us develop our greatest potential toward Christlikeness while we live on earth.

The Truth Explained in Everyday Language

Our life on earth starts with small beginnings. I still find it hard to believe that my 6-foot, 3-inch son once lay in my palms. Life requires constant care at the beginning. Sue and I got very little sleep those first few months as we cared for our baby around the clock. Life requires frequent and balanced nourishment. Kids can eat like bottomless pits; I still wonder where Brent puts it all! Growth comes in small, unnoticed changes. Brent's grandparents, who visit a few times each year, notice his growth better than we do. Growth results in a full-size adult body with maturity.

Jesus said the Christian life begins in new birth, grows, and develops in much the same ways as our children grow and develop physically. Phineas F. Bresee observed, "God's child, like all children, begins a babe. He has to be nursed, fed with milk, cared for, taught, trained, corrected, brought on to manhood."[1] The goal is spiritual maturity. However, growth continues until we go to heaven, where it will continue on a higher level forever. The Bible speaks often about our need to grow and develop in the faith. This prompted Paul to pray in Eph. 3:17-18 that believers, "being rooted and established in love, may have power, together with all the saints, to grasp how wide and long and high and deep is the love of Christ." He further urged that they would not be spiritual infants, swayed by every doctrine that came along. Rather, they were to "grow up into him who is the Head, that is, Christ" (4:15). In Gal. 5:22-23, Paul lists the fruit that a mature Christian should display: "love, joy, peace, patience, kindness, goodness, faithfulness, gentleness and self-control."

**"To acquire self-discipline and self-control,
you start with a single step:
you decide that you can do it."**
—Norman Vincent Peale

Peter addressed a similar concern when he said, "Make every effort to add to your faith goodness; and to goodness, knowledge; and to knowledge, self-control; and to self-control, perseverance; and to perseverance, godliness; and to godliness, brotherly kindness; and to brotherly kindness, love. For if you possess these qualities in increasing measure, they will keep you from being ineffective and unproductive in your knowledge of our Lord Jesus Christ" (2 Pet. 1:5-8).

So what are the elements necessary to the spiritual growth that the Bible outlines? The following is a partial list:

1. *Participate in all the means of grace, such as prayer, Bible reading, meditation, corporate worship, the Lord's Supper, Christian fellowship, and fasting.* An entire chapter will be devoted to these means, so they will not be discussed here. To this list should be added listening to Christian music and reading Christian literature. Make your faith the organizing principle of your life.

2. *Practice the presence of God in your life every day.* Talk with Him throughout the day as you would talk with your closest friend. Listen for His voice directing you, and obey Him. Stop doing what He tells you to stop doing, and start what He tells you to start. Welcome new light from God.

3. *Discipline your life to make it consistent with your commitment to Christ.* This discipline applies to areas like eating habits, enter-

tainment choices, usage of time, choice of friends, responsibility to commitments, keeping of your word, honesty in business dealings, responsibility with your money, and attitudes. Remember the words of Norman Vincent Peale: "To acquire self-discipline and self-control, you start with a single step: you decide that you can do it."[2] You won't always find yourself on top of every situation. Sometimes you will stumble along the way. When you do, talk to the Lord about it, get back up, and keep walking with Christ. Ask Him to help you help yourself.

4. *Learn to cope with life's daily circumstances.* Some days you get the elevator, other days the shaft. Learn not to gauge your level of spiritual maturity on how well things happen to be going at the time. You can be close to God when circumstances are collapsing around you and drifting when everything is going well. Coping skills are as important to successful Christian living as spiritual experiences. Anticipate problems before they become unsolvable. Remember the Russian proverb: "Little drops of water wear down a big stone."[3]

5. *Commit to the Lord your past failures, your appetites, weaknesses, temptations, the failures of others, and situations you cannot change.* Leave all these things in God's hands, and talk to Him about them as often as they come to your mind. Becoming a Christian does not solve all of your problems any more than winning a sweepstakes brings you ultimate happiness. It does give you spiritual resources for dealing effectively with them. Get help from trusted Christian friends or counselors if you need it. God may work through them to help you.

Central to all growth is Christlikeness.

6. *Open all of your life to Kingdom priorities.* This includes giving time and money to the cause of Christ. Give your life away in service to others. It won't seem like an obligation, but rather a welcomed opportunity, as Jesus described in Matt. 25:31-46. His followers fed the hungry, took in strangers, clothed the needy, and cared for the sick and imprisoned without even noticing what they did. It was just a natural outgrowth of their faith. Martin Luther King Jr. reminded, "Everybody can be great . . . because anybody can serve. You only need a heart full of grace. A soul generated by love."[4]

Central to all growth is Christlikeness. Paul says believers have "the mind of Christ" (1 Cor. 2:16). The more time we spend with Him reading His Word and Christian literature, listening to music about Him, and having fellowship with other believers, the more like Him we become. We are adopted into His family, and we take on the family resemblance. It becomes natural for us to prefer the things He prefers and shy away from what displeases Him. Our actions, attitudes, intentions, and motives fall in line with His purposes. As Paul again said, "I want to know Christ and the power of his resurrection and the fellowship of sharing in his sufferings, becoming like him in his death" (Phil. 3:10).

Using the Truth to Enrich Your Life

Christian songs and sermons sometimes put us under bondage about this growth process. You've probably heard the same things I have: "If you don't love Jesus more today than you did yesterday, then you don't love Jesus"; "Life with Jesus gets sweeter every day"; "Christians who live close to God will grow by leaps and bounds." Rather unrealistic, I would say. I can't honestly claim that I feel closer to God today than I did yesterday or that my daily spiritual growth blows the top off the charts. Orel Hershiser said it well: "Christianity is called a spiritual walk. It's not a run and it's not a jog. It's a walk you do from day to day."[5]

I can see growth across the years the same way I watched our child grow. Looking at his annual school pictures proves the point. Snail-paced changes add up. Look back over your spiritual journey since you accepted Christ as your Savior. Have you grown in any of the areas discussed in this chapter? Probably. The "then" and "now" pictures might even be as different as dark and noonday. Don't let the devil defeat you over growth areas that God points out in your life. Let those points of growth serve as proof that you are spiritually alive. God is with you, and He will continue to develop you until the day He calls you home. Remember Phineas F. Bresee's encouragement: "There is no end to the possibilities of a soul in grace. The love of God is measureless, and we may even know more and more of His boundless grace."[6]

Fast Takes

1. Growth occurs slowly in the Christian life, just as it does in physical life.
2. We must do what we can to develop our Christian lives.
3. Christlikeness is the goal of Christian growth.

Prayer

Help me not to get discouraged with my apparent slow rate of growth in Christlikeness, O Lord. Help me to live close to·Your heart and leave the growth analysis to You.

The elect are the "whosoever wills"; the non-elect are the "whosoever won'ts."
—Dwight L. Moody

CHAPTER 15

THE SURE PLAN

PREDESTINATION

Biblical Foundation

"Those God foreknew he also predestined to be conformed to the likeness of his Son, that he might be the firstborn among many brothers. And those he predestined, he also called; those he called, he also justified; those he justified, he also glorified" (Rom. 8:29-30).

"He predestined us to be adopted as his sons through Jesus Christ, in accordance with his pleasure and will. . . . In him we were also chosen, having been predestined according to the plan of him who works out everything in conformity with the purpose of his will" (Eph. 1:5, 11).

At Jesus' birth, angels announced His arrival. They said Christ brought salvation for the whole world, not a select group of individuals chosen by God. The angels brought "good news of great joy that will be for all the people" (Luke 2:10). Jesus came bringing salvation; anyone who trusts in Him receives it.

The Truth Explained in Everyday Language

It's hard to be certain about anything these days. Savings and loan institutions go bankrupt. Politicians break campaign promises. Journalists distort the truth. Military leaders waste money. Retirement funds collapse. Retail businesses close their doors. Sports and religious figures fail morally. Our favorite soft drink goes off the market. We learn to live with a sense of uncertainty, maybe even skepticism.

I'll never forget Brent's comment as a small child to a particular advertising claim: "Don't believe it, Dad—that's *not* true!" How quickly they learn!

While uncertainty may be characteristic of household names and products, God does not want us to have any doubts about His plan to save us—not even optimistic skepticism. His Word presents His plan in very certain terms. A biblical word used to describe that plan is "predestination." It means "to mark out beforehand." A great deal of discussion and disagreement in church history have centered around exactly what is marked out beforehand. Some say God preselects those who are invited to receive salvation. This preselected process has two explanations. One explanation says everyone deserves to go to hell, but out of His mercy God selects some from the damned to go to heaven. Theologians call this "single predestination." The other explanation says He selects some people for heaven and others for hell. In other words, God prepares a "saved" list and a "damned" one. Theologians call this "double predestination." Others deny preselection views entirely and say the eternal destiny of any who accept God's plan is guaranteed. In other words, predestination does not determine who gets picked for salvation, but rather what happens to those who accept God's salvation offer.

**Yes, God is sovereign, and He has power
over everything in all creation,
but He has chosen to limit himself
at the point of our free will.**

Those teaching preselection views base their ideas on two assumptions. First, they strongly emphasize God's sovereignty or all-powerfulness. He's the Boss—He can do anything He wants to do. Second, they say Christ died on the Cross for those whom God selected, not for everyone. Otherwise, God's plan fails if Christ died for people who do not accept Him. Since God's plans are perfect and cannot fail, God obviously didn't plan for those to be saved in the first place.

Both assumptions are faulty. Yes, God is certainly sovereign, and He has power over everything in all creation, but He has chosen to limit himself at the point of our free will. No doubt He could disregard our freedom if He chose to do so. But He does not treat us as hand puppets or checkerboard pieces. He respects our right to choose to serve Him or not. No, Christ did not die on the Cross only for those whom God selected. The Bible clearly teaches that Christ died for everyone. Jesus told Nicodemus that the plan was for "whoever believes in him" (John 3:16). He told His disciples to preach the gospel throughout the world and make disciples of all nations (Matt. 24:14; 28:19). If God loves everyone in the world (John 3:16) and does not wish for anyone to perish (2 Pet. 3:9), then it stands to reason that Christ died to make salvation a possibility for everyone.

**Everyone who has faith in Christ,
who simply trusts Him for salvation,
is guaranteed a place in heaven.**

A better interpretation of Scripture, then, says predestination does not determine who is picked for salvation but what happens to those who accept God's offer for salvation. Everyone who has faith in Christ, who simply trusts Him for salvation, is guaranteed a place in heaven. We live our lives on this earth "in Christ" (1 Cor. 1:2; 2 Cor. 5:17; Col. 1:28) and become more Christlike in character and conduct (Rom. 8:29). When we reach life's end, our faith and hope are rewarded with eternal salvation.

We must always remember that God offers salvation as a gift. But He does not predetermine or force our choice. Prevenient grace opens our eyes to our spiritual need. Yet we must exercise free will and choose to accept His gift. From the time we accept Christ until we go to heaven to be with Him forever, we are daily recipients of His inexhaustible generosity. This road we travel with God is neither uncharted nor uncertain. God has a predetermined plan to bring us safely home.

Using the Truth to Enrich Your Life

A city bus passes in front of my office every day. The sign on the front of it reads "Downtown." The bus driver does not carry a list of who can ride the bus; everyone with a dollar bill is welcome. Neither does he drive wherever his imagination takes him each day. He has a predetermined travel plan that takes the bus from our suburb to the center of the city. If I choose to get on that bus, the bus company guarantees that I will end up downtown. I am not forced to stay on the bus all the way to its final destination. I can pull the cord over the window and get off any time I want. But if I choose to stay with my original decision, I will get downtown sooner or later. (Probably later, knowing that bus's tendency to get behind schedule!)

That's the way predestination works. The bus of salvation passes by our heart. Jesus Christ sits in the driver's seat. The sign on the front reads "Heaven." The driver does not have a predetermined list of riders; He invites everyone to come aboard. If we choose to get on the bus, God guarantees that we will end up in heaven. We are not forced to stay on the bus all the way to its final destination. We can get off any time we want. But if we choose to stay with our original decision, we are certain to make it to heaven someday.

In a world of uncertainty, that's one thing for sure!

Fast Takes

1. Predestination means "to mark out beforehand."
2. Everyone who has faith in Christ for salvation is guaranteed a place in heaven.
3. God offers us the gift but does not force our choice.

Prayer

I bow in humble gratitude for Your certain plan of salvation, O God.

CHRISTIAN LIFE

*The holiest moment of the church service is the
moment when God's people—strengthened by
preaching and sacrament—go out of the
church door into the world to be the Church.
We didn't go to church; we are the Church.*
                    —Canon Ernest Southcott

CHAPTER 16

THE BODY OF CHRIST ON EARTH

THE CHURCH

Biblical Foundation

> *"Simon Peter answered, 'You are the Christ, the Son of the liv-
> ing God.'... 'You are Peter, and on this rock I will build my church,
> and the gates of Hades will not overcome it'"* (Matt. 16:16, 18).

> *"God placed all things under his feet and appointed him to be
> head over everything for the church, which is his body, the fullness
> of him who fills everything in every way"* (Eph. 1:22-23).

Jesus talked throughout His public ministry of bringing the kingdom of God to earth. He said those who heard His preaching would
see it come in their lifetime. Then, just before He returned to His Father, He told His disciples to wait together in Jerusalem for the Holy
Spirit to come to them. The fulfillment of that promise on the Day of
Pentecost brought the birthday of the Church, the continuation of
God's kingdom on earth.

The Truth Explained in Everyday Language

Jesus Christ came to earth to give us an insider's view of the Father's love and to establish our personal relationship with Him. When

the time came for His return to the Father, He made provision for bonding His disciples together in a special organization. This organization became known as the Church—those who are called out from the world to serve Christ. Jesus told Peter the Church would be built on his confession of faith: "You are the Christ, the Son of the living God" (Matt. 16:16). Jesus used a play on words in His discussion with Peter. He told Peter *(Petros)* that He would build His Church on a large rock *(petra)*, thus on Peter's confession and not Peter himself. The Christian Church is not just a human organization; its strength and authority come from Christ.

The Christian Church is not just a human organization; its strength and authority come from Christ.

The Church is not a building; it meets together *in* buildings. The Church is the Body of Believers who confess Jesus Christ as the Son of God and trust in Him for their salvation. This Body unites together under Christ's leadership and so is called "the body of Christ" (1 Cor. 12:27; Eph. 1:22-23). Christ is the Head; believers are the hands and feet to do His work on earth. Each of the members is connected and must work together like the human body to show God to the world. Phineas F. Bresee once said, "The one way that Christ can be seen and felt is in and through His people."[1] That is the significance of the French proverb that says, "A church is God between four walls."[2] The Body life concept is also taught in Rom. 12, 1 Cor. 12, Eph. 4, and Col. 1.

Body life reminds us that the church is more than an organization of individual believers. The Holy Spirit knits these believers together to form an organism. This organism functions in a number of ways: worshiping God, preaching the Word of God, celebrating the sacraments, studying the faith, having fellowship, sharing time and money with the needy, and evangelizing the lost. Members work together and depend upon one another, like police officers partnered together. They balance the strengths and weaknesses of each other, like a husband-and-wife team. They provide mutual support and encouragement, like an accountability partner.

The benefits of the Church extend beyond this life. Its highest calling involves preparing people for eternity. Henry Ward Beecher's observation regarding the Church serves as an important reminder: "The church is not a gallery for the exhibition of eminent Christians, but a school for the education of imperfect ones, a nursery for the care of weak ones, a hospital for the healing of those who need special care."[3]

Paul also referred to the Church as "the people of God." In 2 Cor. 6:16 he said, "We are the temple of the living God. As God has said: 'I will live with them and walk among them, and I will be their God, and they will be my people.'" We must not dilute our Christian faith with any other allegiance; God expects our undivided loyalty. He repays that loyalty by working among us in special ways, as a parent works with his or her child. God also reminds us in this passage that He expects us to live holy lives, unpolluted by the world's sinful influences. We are to live "a cut above."

The Church manifests the kingdom of God on earth; every group of believers represents a "branch office."

Jesus came to earth not only to give us an insider's view of the Father's love but also to establish the kingdom of God among us (Mark 1:15). His life and ministry focused on building that Kingdom. What is a kingdom? We often think of a landmass, a monarch, or a castle. But a kingdom is none of these. Rather, it involves people subject to a ruler. So the kingdom of God exists anywhere you find people who give God control of their lives. That's what we mean when we pray the portion of the Lord's Prayer that says, "Your kingdom come, your will be done on earth as it is in heaven" (Matt. 6:10). We are asking God to help us do His will in our lives as fully as it is done in heaven. The Church, then, manifests the kingdom of God on earth. Every group of believers represents a "branch office."

Jesus left His disciples to carry on His work of building the kingdom of God, organized together in the Church. That's the reason He told them, "You will receive power when the Holy Spirit comes on you; and you will be my witnesses in Jerusalem, and in all Judea and Samaria, and to the ends of the earth" (Acts 1:8). God fulfilled that promise on the Day of Pentecost when the Holy Spirit filled believers. The Book of Acts records the miraculous growth of the Church and the spread of the Christian faith in the years immediately following Pentecost. Growth has continued from then until now.

Often critics look at the Church with its flaws and problems and conclude that it has drifted far from its roots. Not true. The Book of Acts and most of Paul's Epistles document all manner of problems in the Early Church. Anytime a group of imperfect people come together, problems soon follow. As the old evangelist said, "The only way to have a perfect church is to throw out all of the current members and don't take any new ones in."

The genius of the Church is not that it is trouble-free, but that the Holy Spirit works to resolve the problems. The world should see a difference in the way we live and love. When asked to give the Church's best witness to the world, John Wesley said, "Outlive them; outlove them; outdie them." God can give us the power to do just that.

For all of the differences between believers, they are mostly united around the preaching of the Word, the Lordship of Christ, and the observance of baptism and Communion. They witness to the world of the life-changing power of God and participate in God's mission to help hurting humanity. They anxiously anticipate the day God calls them home and fulfills the vision of Paul when he said, "Christ loved the church and gave himself up for her to make her holy, cleansing her by the washing with water through the word, and to present her to himself as a radiant church, without stain or wrinkle or any other blemish, but holy and blameless" (Eph. 5:25-27). The Church is not perfect yet, but it will be.

Using the Truth to Enrich Your Life

I teach a Sunday School class at my church. The people in that class amaze me. They represent a cross section of the Body of Christ. Some are new Christians; others have been in the faith most of their lives. Some love to speak up in class; others are shy and never say a word. Some have deep insights into the Scriptures; others have a lot to learn. Some are wealthy; others barely have enough money to meet financial obligations. Some are businesspeople. Others are housewives. Still others are retired from work. Some are young, others older.

Week after week we gather around the Word of God. We share ideas, agreeing on some things and disagreeing on others. Class members do not take offense with one another when they do not see eye to eye on particular points of the discussion. We share one another's burdens, rejoicing over answered prayer and praying over needs. We laugh and cry together. We send one another cards in the mail, call one another on the telephone, and visit in one another's homes. Occasionally we get together in the church fellowship hall or local park for a class dinner and fellowship.

When I think of my Sunday School class and my church, I am reminded of Acts 2:42—"They devoted themselves to the apostles' teaching and to the fellowship, to the breaking of bread and to prayer." Life takes us in a dozen different directions throughout the week, but on Sunday, Christians unite to share Christ's life. Christ is in each of our hearts, and we share His Spirit together.

Fast Takes

1. The Church is composed of those who are called out from the world to serve Christ.

2. The Church is the Body of Christ; Christ is the Head, and we are the hands and feet to help build God's kingdom in human lives.
3. The Holy Spirit gives the Church life and power.
4. God will ultimately make the Church holy and blameless.

Prayer

Thank You, God, for making me part of Your kingdom on earth. Work through me to accomplish Your will in Your world.

Come, Holy Spirit, Dove divine,
On these baptismal waters shine,
And teach our hearts, in highest strain,
To praise the Lamb for sinners slain.
—Adoniram Judson

CHAPTER 17

THE PROMISE

BAPTISM

Biblical Foundation

"When the people heard this, they were cut to the heart and said to Peter and the other apostles, 'Brothers, what shall we do?' Peter replied, 'Repent and be baptized, every one of you, in the name of Jesus Christ for the forgiveness of your sins. And you will receive the gift of the Holy Spirit'" (Acts 2:37-38).

"He saved us, not because of righteous things we had done, but because of his mercy. He saved us through the washing of re-birth and renewal by the Holy Spirit" (Titus 3:5).

John the Baptist baptized his cousin Jesus in a public Jordan River ceremony. This event marked the beginning of Jesus' public ministry. It also marked the Father's first public announcement of His blessing on His Son's ministry. This high and holy moment became a significant event for Jesus.

The Truth Explained in Everyday Language

Symbols add meaning to daily life. We shake hands with people when we agree on a business deal or meet someone new. We cut a big ribbon when we open a shopping center or a new highway. We burn the mortgage when we make the last house or church building payment. We lay hands on people at church when we pray for their healing or ordain them into ministry. We raise a hand in the worship service to indicate agreement or a special spiritual moment. Symbols help us communicate more than words can express. They often mark a moment in time we will remember for a few days or a lifetime.

Baptism is one of the central symbols of the Christian faith.

Baptism is one of the central symbols of the Christian faith. It symbolizes a number of spiritual truths. Here are a few of them:

1. Baptism symbolizes new birth. It tells everyone a radical spiritual transaction has occurred.
2. Baptism symbolizes that God has washed our sins away, just as a bath washes dirt from our bodies. This is what Paul meant in Titus 3:5, quoted above.
3. Baptism symbolizes the coming of the Holy Spirit into our lives. With the stain of sin washed away, our hearts become a clean place for the Spirit to live in. Paul said in 1 Cor. 3:16 that we are God's temple and that His Spirit lives in us.
4. Baptism symbolizes that God will be faithful to His end of the contract to save us just as He promised. He saves us from our sinful life now and takes us to heaven when we die. God once gave another symbol—the rainbow—which was His promise not to destroy the world with another flood.
5. Baptism symbolizes entering into a contract with God and pledging ourselves to be faithful to the Christian faith. It replaces the Old Testament symbol of circumcision.
6. Baptism symbolizes the completion of a spiritual transaction with God. Something has happened both from God's perspective and ours. It is an event in time, not a process throughout life—the same way we were dry one moment and wet the next. Sure, we will grow in the grace of God, but we have passed through the doorway and into the room of salvation.
7. Baptism symbolizes a water grave in which we die with Christ. As we come up out of the water, we are raised to new life in Christ. Paul gives an extended explanation of this idea in Rom. 6:1-11. As he says in verse 4, "We were therefore buried with him through baptism into death in order that, just as Christ was raised from the dead through the glory of the Father, we too may live a new life."

Jesus instituted baptism as the outward sign for all these spiritual messages. Because He placed such significance on it, we call it a "sacrament." That simply means a special outward symbol for spiritual grace. Baptism did not debut as a new religious symbol in Jesus' day. Other religions in the Middle East used it to initiate new members. Some of them used animal blood instead of water. John the Baptist baptized those who joined his group. His most significant candidate was Jesus Christ (Matt. 3:13-17).

Baptism symbolizes a water grave in which we die with Christ.

Obviously Jesus did not need this experience to establish a new spiritual relationship with the Father. He was not a sinner; He did not need to repent and change His ways. So why did He insist against John's objections on being baptized? For us—to give us an example and remind us of baptism's importance. Had He not been baptized, we might have gotten the idea that He did not value it. Jesus got baptized, and so should we.

Not only did Jesus give us His example, but also He directed us to baptize people when they became Christians. He included baptism in His Great Commission: "Therefore go and make disciples of all nations, baptizing them in the name of the Father and of the Son and of the Holy Spirit, and teaching them to obey everything I have commanded you. And surely I am with you always, to the very end of the age" (Matt. 28:19-20). The Early Church gave baptism an important place, as indicated in Peter's sermon on the Day of Pentecost (Acts 2:37-38, quoted above). The New Testament mentions it frequently as a ritual of the Christian faith.

The Bible does not, however, specify a particular mode of baptism. Some ministers sprinkle water on believers' heads as they stand before a Christian congregation. Others pour a pitcher of water over believers' heads as they stand in a church baptistery or an outdoor body of water. Still others completely immerse believers in a pool of water either in the church baptistery or outside. Since the Bible does not specify, any of these methods is acceptable. We should not criticize those who do it differently than we do.

While some people teach that the act of baptism itself saves a person, it is not a commonly accepted view. Most Christians believe the personal faith of accepting Jesus Christ saves a person. Baptism symbolizes that simple trust. No faith, no salvation—baptism or not.

Should infants be baptized? Some think we should baptize them to symbolize their incorporation into the covenant community of faith; others fear baptism creates a false sense of security and believe we should wait until children are old enough to accept Christ personally. The latter group prefers the ritual of infant dedication. In both infant baptism and dedication, the parents and Christian community are admonished to assume their responsibility to raise this child in the Christian faith and lead him or her to a personal knowledge of Christ. The only difference is that infant dedication does not use water in the ritual. Infant baptism is acceptable as long as parents, and later the child, do not assume it replaces a personal acceptance of Christ as Savior. Many times baptized infants wish to be baptized again as young persons or adults, symbolizing their personal commitment to Christ. This personal choice is also acceptable.

Using the Truth to Enrich Your Life

I like to save remembrances from important occasions. I have several boxes of pictures, brochures, canceled admission tickets, and greeting cards that record a lifetime of special experiences. Sue thinks I'm a pack rat. I occasionally look back through these items and recall the emotions surrounding each of them.

One of those remembrances is a card my pastor gave me at my baptism. This marked a significant spiritual moment. When I look at that card, I recall all that the ritual of baptism symbolizes. I drove down a stake in my life that day as I testified to the world that I belonged to Christ. I determined to live the rest of my life for Him. My commitment glows as brightly today as it did those many years ago. My baptism was a deeply meaningful experience; God did something for me in that ritual that I've never gotten over. Nothing magical, but it said more than mere words could express. I made God a promise that day, and He made me a promise as well. Because He's been faithful to me, I've been faithful to Him. It will be that way until He takes me home. How do I know? He promised!

Fast Takes

1. Symbols add meaning to life by communicating more than words can say.
2. Baptism symbolizes all that is involved in becoming a Christian.
3. Baptism cannot save a person; only faith in Christ can do that.

Prayer

Thank You, God, for this special symbol of Your promise of new birth and eternal life.

Here, O my Lord, I see Thee face to face;
 Here would I touch and handle things unseen;
Here grasp with firmer hand eternal grace,
 And all my weariness upon Thee lean.
                                    —Horatius Bonar

CHAPTER 18

A REMEMBRANCE AND A FORETASTE

THE LORD'S SUPPER

Biblical Foundation

"He took bread, gave thanks and broke it, and gave it to them, saying, 'This is my body given for you; do this in remembrance of me.' In the same way, after the supper he took the cup, saying, 'This cup is the new covenant in my blood, which is poured out for you'" (Luke 22:19-20).

"Whenever you eat this bread and drink this cup, you proclaim the Lord's death until he comes" (1 Cor. 11:26).

Jesus gathered His disciples together on the night of His betrayal and shared one last meal with them—the Passover feast. He took two parts of that ceremony, eating unleavened bread and drinking wine, and applied them to His particular situation. From that day to this, His disciples have remembered that night with a rehearsal of His ceremony.

The Truth Explained in Everyday Language

Some rituals of our faith may be observed only once in a lifetime, as with baptism. Other rituals are observed often, as with the Lord's Supper. We also call this ritual "Communion" or "Eucharist." "Communion" means "fellowship" or "participation." We experience a special fellowship with the Lord when we take Communion. "Eucharist" means "giving thanks." Thus, we offer the Lord an enactment of our thankfulness for salvation. The phrase "Lord's Supper" reminds us of the evening of His betrayal.

Christ's sacrifice far surpasses the requirements of the Old Testament sacrificial system, because it gives us a clear conscience with God.

The Lord's Supper along with baptism are the two chief sacraments recognized almost universally in the Christian faith. The Lord's Supper symbolizes several spiritual truths. Here are a few:

1. The bread represents the body of Christ, the juice His blood. His body was broken and His blood spilled for our salvation. Blood symbolizes life, so the spilling of blood symbolizes giving life away. Thus, the Lord's Supper memorializes His death (1 Cor. 11:26).

2. As stated in the Atonement discussion, Christ's death completed the Old Testament sacrificial system. He became our Passover Lamb, sacrificed for our sins (1 Cor. 5:7). Heb. 9:11-28 gives a full presentation of this subject. Especially helpful is verse 14: "How much more, then, will the blood of Christ, who through the eternal Spirit offered himself unblemished to God, cleanse our consciences from acts that lead to death, so that we may serve the living God!" Christ's sacrifice far surpasses the requirements of the Old Testament sacrificial system, because it gives us a clear conscience with God. That clear conscience is reaffirmed every time we participate in this special meal.

3. The Lord's Supper is also a promise of God that He will bring us all together again someday to celebrate the Marriage Supper of the Lamb with Christ as honored Guest and Host. This will happen at the end of time. During His last meal with His disciples, Jesus promised, "I tell you, I will not drink of this fruit of the vine from now on until that day when I drink it anew with you in my Father's kingdom" (Matt. 26:29). John saw a vision during God's Revelation to him of that meal we will share together (Rev. 19:9). What a feast it will be, not because of the menu, but because of Jesus' presence!

4. We participate in this ritual as a testimony to our faith in Christ and a spiritual renewal. Eating and drinking remind us that our spirits receive spiritual strength from God the same way our bodies receive physical strength from eating food. That's why

some Christians take Communion every day or every week, though most receive it less frequently. Grace is not literally contained in the physical elements; it remains a spiritual matter.

5. Christ is present in this ritual in a special way. We do not believe the bread and juice actually become the literal body and blood of Christ, as some teach. However, we do believe this ritual gives God a special opportunity to speak to our spirits and work in our hearts in a unique way. God speaks through Communion similarly to the way He speaks through a sermon, prayer, or Bible reading.

Communion is not for everyone. Scripture implies that the ritual is for Christians. However, an unbeliever ready to become a Christian could accept Christ as Savior during a time of heart preparation prior to the ritual and receive it as a testimony to newfound faith.

Paul indicated that believers should prepare their hearts prior to taking Communion (1 Cor. 11:27-32). He specifically said, "A man ought to examine himself before he eats of the bread and drinks of the cup" (v. 28). This verse does not mean we should decline participating because of some unknown failure or sin. I have known overly sensitive people who so feared unworthiness that they never received Communion. Their response caused them to miss a special blessing from God. Paul's admonition means we should not be casual in our attitude toward Communion. As we prayerfully examine our hearts, God will reveal any failure in our spiritual lives. This spiritual checkup allows God an opportunity to update us regularly on our relationship with Him.

Should children be served Communion? The Bible does not give specific direction, so it is a personal choice. However, I feel children should be served Communion as soon as they are old enough to understand its meaning. The ceremony provides parents a wonderful opportunity to teach their children spiritual truth. Sue and I served Brent as a small child. He felt included in this special Christian ceremony; in fact, it became his favorite Christian ritual. As a child, he got excited when he saw the Communion trays displayed at the front of the sanctuary. The time eventually comes when parents can use the ritual to present their children the plan of salvation.

As to the elements to be used for Communion, the Bible is specific. The Jewish Passover feast used unleavened bread and wine. Almost everyone uses some form of unleavened bread, though other forms of bread are acceptable. Grape juice has replaced wine in many churches today, in order to abstain from alcohol. The wine of Jesus' day was probably not fermented with as high an alcoholic content as wines today.

How often should Christians take Communion? Often enough for the ritual to provide spiritual benefit and an opportunity to grow in grace but not so frequently that we take it for granted. I personally think every day or every week may be too often; once a year is not often enough. At least once every three months is the established rule in my denomination, but I prefer once a month.

Using the Truth to Enrich Your Life

Relationships with one another deepen when we eat together. We can eat steak in a nice restaurant or hot dogs around a campfire. The food and location do not matter. In many cultures, a sign of closest friendship comes by inviting someone to eat in your home. We tend to let down our defenses and be ourselves when we eat together. Sue and I often have friends into our home for a meal. Christian fellowship adds rich meaning to life. So it's fitting that one of the central rituals of the Christian faith involves eating a special meal in God's house.

This meal reminds us vividly how much the Father loves us: enough to send His Son to die on the Cross for us.

This meal reminds us vividly how much the Father loves us: enough to send His Son to die on the Cross for us. It reminds us of the close fellowship He desires to have with us. It reminds us of our need for spiritual checkups from time to time. It reminds us of the unity of believers in the Christian community. And it reminds us of our hope of heaven and the time we will sit down with Jesus at the Marriage Supper of the Lamb. What a feast that will be! It will mark the beginning of life with God forever.

So the next time you partake of Communion with fellow believers, remember the awesome significance of the ritual, and allow God to draw you closer to His side and remind you of His incomprehensible love.

Fast Takes

1. The Lord's Supper reminds us of Christ's sacrifice on the Cross for our salvation and of His coming again.
2. When we participate in the Lord's Supper, we testify to our faith in Christ and receive spiritual renewal and strength from Him.
3. The Lord's Supper should be taken often enough to provide spiritual benefit but not so often that we take it for granted.

Prayer

Thank You, God, for another special reminder of Your constant love and spiritual renewal. Keep me until we sit together at Your special banquet.

Grace is but glory begun and glory is but grace perfected.

—Jonathan Edwards

CHAPTER 19

CHANNELS OF GOD'S GRACE

MEANS OF GRACE

Biblical Foundation

"For it is by grace you have been saved, through faith—and this not from yourselves, it is the gift of God—not by works, so that no one can boast" (Eph. 2:8-9).

"[God] has saved us and called us to a holy life—not because of anything we have done but because of his own purpose and grace. This grace was given us in Christ Jesus before the beginning of time" (2 Tim. 1:9).

Jesus came to earth not just to tell us about the Father, but to show us how to connect our lives to His. Jesus became a living example for us, a model to follow. When we look at His life, we see Him doing all the things we can do to draw close to God and find His grace for our lives. As in every other area of the Christian life, Jesus pioneered the way.

The Truth Explained in Everyday Language

I remember God's grace every month when I pay our family bills. Not because God drops money out of the sky to pay them—I wish He did. No, I think of God's grace because most of our bills have a "grace period" for payment. That means I can pay them 10 to 14 days after the due date without a penalty. I didn't ask my creditors for it; they just gave it to me. I usually don't need the grace period. I do use it, however, around Christmas and summer vacation time when expenses increase. My creditors have no obligation to extend grace to me; they do it as a service to their customers.

God's grace parallels this analogy in several ways. Most importantly, we do not deserve it. Nothing we have done or ever will do can make us worthy. Nothing obligates God to give us grace; He does it because He loves us. Though always available, we must find ways to apply it to daily life. That's the focus of this chapter—God's channels of grace.

In many ways, our salvation requires cooperation. God provides the plan and the methods to accomplish that plan, but we must step in His direction by accepting His offer. This in no way implies earning salvation. It simply means we do not passively sit and watch God do everything for us. As the farmers back home say, "God gives the grain, but we must make the furrow." For example, He offers forgiveness for our sins, but we must ask Him for it. Otherwise, it remains like an unopened present under the Christmas tree the day after Christmas. In that same way, God offers us His help, but we must put forth the effort to accept it. As the old-timers put it, "We take one step toward God; He comes the rest of the way to us."

**Meditation provides us
with a quiet time for God to speak
to us and bring us deeper understanding.**

The following are channels of God's grace in daily living. I am using John Wesley's outline of direct and indirect means of grace. Let's look first at the direct means:

1. *Prayer.* We bow our heads and our hearts before God and communicate directly with Him. Prayer includes praise and adoration for who God is, confession of our faults and failures, thanksgiving for what God has done for us, and petition for our needs and those on our prayer list. While talking with God, He is able to remind us of His favor and love. An entire chapter follows on this subject.
2. *Bible reading.* The Bible is more than an ancient record of God's acts in history. It is also a living letter for today. When we read it, we hear fresh words from God communicated to our hearts by the Holy Spirit. We learn more about our faith, about God's plan of salvation, about the ways He has worked in the lives of other believers, and about our eternal destiny. We also learn how to put this information to work in the trenches of life. On almost every page of the Bible, we read of God's favor toward us.
3. *Meditation.* After we've read God's Word and perhaps a devo-

tional thought, and we've said all that's on our hearts to say to Him, we must take time to allow our heart and mind to reflect on God's truth. Meditation provides us with a quiet time for God to speak to us and bring us deeper understanding. God has a difficult time teaching us with our minds spinning in high gear all the time. We can even fall into the trap of remaining in high gear during our devotions, like racing a car engine with the transmission in park. Meditation slows us down and lets God's grace soak deep into our being, like a soft rain on a spring day. Meditation has no instant or accelerated modes—it takes time.

4. *Corporate worship*. Salvation is not entirely an individual matter. True, we are solely responsible for choosing to follow God or not. And we will answer to God for our personal lives. But we live as members of a community of faith. Each represents one part of a body. God's presence comes in special ways during corporate worship. Jesus said, "For where two or three come together in my name, there am I with them" (Matt. 18:20). The reason for this is because God lives in each of our hearts. When we come together to worship Him, a special connection resonates between believers. God communicates through the entire group.

5. *The Lord's Supper*. We have already discussed the special ways God reaches out to us in the unique worship opportunity of the Lord's Supper. Mere words cannot say all that is conveyed through the activity of touching, smelling, tasting, and eating the Communion elements. Everything connected with this ritual speaks of salvation's benefits.

6. *Christian fellowship*. God sometimes speaks to us through the words and actions of other Christians. It is important to meet together often, for as Reuben Welch says, "We really do need each other." We support one another and share burdens. We make ourselves accountable to one another and responsible to keep one another faithful to our Christian commitment. God's grace works through the entire group, drawing us closer to one another and to Him.

7. *Fasting*. This spiritual exercise involves denying the body food for a certain period of time. Scripture does not require it as an essential activity. We do it when we're carrying a heavy burden, needing God's direction, or asking for His help in a particular matter. The focus is so keen or the need so great that we would rather pray than eat. We may even lose our appetite for food. Jesus gave specific fasting instructions in the Sermon on the Mount (Matt. 6:16-18). Chief among them—don't fast to impress others, but to seek God's help.

The indirect means of grace include the following:

1. *Discipline.* We must bring every part of our lives under the control of Christ. This includes our physical and mental appetites, our emotional needs, our mood swings, our speech, and our use of material resources. Paul said, "I beat my body and make it my slave so that after I have preached to others, I myself will not be disqualified for the prize" (1 Cor. 9:27). As an old preacher said, "He is not fit to command others who cannot command himself." We learn more about God's grace as we bring all of life under the Lordship of Christ.

**When we get our hands
dirty in God's service,
we experience His grace
in special ways.**

2. *Service.* Albert Schweitzer reminded us, "The only ones . . . who will be really happy are those who have sought and found how to serve."[1] We have a responsibility not only to look after our individual salvation but also to give our lives away in service to others. Our faith should always reach out to the needy. We should seek the same compassionate heart Jesus demonstrated in His earthly ministry. When we get our hands dirty in God's service, we experience His grace in special ways. Phineas F. Bresee said, "Instead of taking a man out of service and burden-bearing for men, the religion of Jesus makes him the servant of all, and as far as possible he bears the burdens of all."[2]

3. *Suffering.* None of us ask for times of suffering in our lives. In fact, if the choice were ours, we would probably choose to avoid as much suffering as possible. However, suffering can be good for soul making. It can help grow our faith and draw us closer to His side. When we look back over a difficult time in life, we often see God walking beside us or carrying us. These times can be great opportunities for Him to display special grace. Remember Grandma's words from the heat of life's battles: "Crosses are ladders that lead to heaven."

Using the Truth to Enrich Your Life

Last week in my night class a student asked a series of questions that went something like this: "Where is God when I need Him?" "Why doesn't He work in our world like in Bible times?" "Why doesn't He communicate with us?" He just couldn't see God working in the world. He saw only with his physical eyes and heard only with his physical ears. I took a lot of class time trying to explain how Christians learn to recognize God's presence and work in a variety of ways.

The means of grace we have explored are all ways God comes, works, and communicates in our lives. He involves himself as much as we allow Him. He seeks daily to reach us with messages of concern and energy for the task.

For your own spiritual growth and development, do the following exercise for a week or two. Be attentive to all of the clues of God's love and grace. Write them down. Look over your list at the end of the exercise, and see the varied ways God uses to communicate with us. Then make it a daily practice to be sensitive and open to His tender voice. Learn to hear and respond to Him.

Fast Takes

1. God finds ways to reach out to us every day with His grace.
2. We are responsible to make the effort to receive this grace.
3. We must learn to recognize God's reminders of His love and be sensitive to His voice.

Prayer

Help me, God, to open myself to Your channels of grace and see Your work in my life today.

To clasp the hands in prayer is the beginning of an uprising against the disorder of the world.

—Karl Barth

CHAPTER 20

A FRIEND IN HIGH PLACES

PRAYER

Biblical Foundation

"Our Father in heaven, hallowed be your name, your kingdom come, your will be done on earth as it is in heaven. Give us today our daily bread. Forgive us our debts, as we also have forgiven our debtors. And lead us not into temptation, but deliver us from the evil one" (Matt. 6:9-13).

"Father, if you are willing, take this cup from me; yet not my will, but yours be done" (Luke 22:42).

Jesus gave an important place to prayer in His everyday life. He talked to the Father as freely as He talked to His friends; in fact, He probably talked to Him more than He talked to His friends. His example reminds us that prayer is an essential part of life, as important as eating, drinking, exercising, and sleeping. If Jesus found prayer to be so helpful, how much more should we realize its benefits?

The Truth Explained in Everyday Language

Jesus' prayer life must have been contagious, because His disciples wanted to learn how to pray as He did (Luke 11:1). He presented prayer as personal communication with the Father. It is as varied as communication with other people.

● Sometimes we pray to praise God for who He is. At other times we wish to thank Him for what He has done or is doing in our world or our lives.

- Sometimes we bring to God the needs of friends or loved ones. At other times we come with our own needs.
- Sometimes we have an inner desire for fellowship with our Creator and Friend. At other times we're driven to prayer by an emergency or difficult situation.
- Sometimes we pray for adequate strength for the task at hand. At other times we are completely overwhelmed by a sense of our own inability to do anything right.
- Sometimes we pray with well-formed sentences and carefully selected words. At other times our prayers are nothing more than groans and cries for help.

Jesus taught us almost everything we know about prayer. He modeled many prayer principles for His followers. He directed us to pray as naturally as we breathe (Luke 18:1). He said prayer's purpose is fellowship with God, not to impress others with our ability to articulate words (Matt 6:7).

Jesus taught us to come often and stay as long as we can.

Essential elements for a successful prayer life appear in the Lord's Prayer found in Matt. 6. Personal prayer is a private matter, not a public performance (v. 5). We are to approach God as our Heavenly Father (v. 9). We must reverence and honor Him (v. 9). We pledge ourselves to live as citizens of His kingdom while on this earth and follow His will as carefully as the angels in heaven follow it (v. 10). We recognize our dependence upon Him for life's provisions (v. 11). We need His forgiveness of our sins and shortcomings, and we need to manifest this same forgiving attitude toward those who fail us (v. 12). God will be disposed toward forgiving and helping us in the same way we are disposed toward those who do us wrong (v. 14). We recognize the power and pull of temptation and seek His help in resisting it (v. 13). Finally, we need God's help in maintaining victory over Satan and all the forces of evil (v. 13).

During His earthly ministry, Jesus often talked with His Father. He drew away from the crowds or spent the early morning hours in prayer (Luke 6:12). He waited before the Father prior to every big decision, such as the selection of His disciples (v. 13). No matter how busy His schedule kept Him, He did not allow it to crowd out His time with the Father (Mark 6:46). He prayed conversationally, the way

He talked with His friends (John 17:1-26). He unburdened His heart but then asked the Father to answer as He saw best (Luke 22:42).

Regardless of the reason we come to God and regardless of the words we use when we get there, He welcomes us with open arms and says, "Come now, let us reason together" (Isa. 1:18). He loves for us to come to Him, and He delights in talking with us while we are together. Jesus taught us to come often and stay as long as we can.

Prayer is one of the rare privileges of life. Other world religions pray to their gods, but Christian prayer is different. For the followers of these other gods, prayer is a one-way street—they talk but do not receive a direct answer. It is like dropping a letter into the mailbox. Prayers are offered to appease the gods' anger or win favor. By contrast, Christians and Jews see prayer as a two-way street, with God both hearing and answering, like talking on the telephone. It is a time of intimate friendship.

I recently saw a bumper sticker that read, "Don't bother praying. God already knows everything." Yes, God does know everything, but the purpose of prayer is not to inform Him of our situation. What is prayer's purpose, then?

1. Prayer helps us properly assess and clarify our situation. Our problem may seem large and undefined before we pray about it. Prayer focuses the picture, similar to fine-tuning a TV set.

2. Prayer helps put the situation in perspective. Our problem may seem like the biggest thing in the world before we pray about it. Prayer lets the air out of our inflated problem, as when air is released from a balloon.

3. Prayer reminds us that we are not facing our situation alone. God is with us and helping us. He partners with us and comes to stand beside us, like a friend coming to our aid.

4. Prayer gives us an opportunity to talk with Someone about our situation. We need a listening ear to bare our soul to and share our burden with. He is better than a stranger on the bus or even our most trusted friend.

5. Prayer places us in the right attitude or frame of mind to see matters from God's perspective. We often come to Him from a self-centered perspective. Time in prayer turns us around so we can see things from His point of view.

6. Prayer gives God the opportunity to work in our lives or in circumstances in ways that He would not do if we did not pray. The all-powerful Creator of the universe chooses to work through us as we open ourselves to His will and purpose. It opens channels for God's involvement. As Phillips Brooks wisely reminds, "Prayer is not conquering God's reluctance but taking hold of God's willingness."[1]

Using the Truth to Enrich Your Life

Several people in my Sunday School class are full-fledged prayer warriors. They have fought and won many of life's battles on their knees. I love to hear them pray. I feel as though I'm listening in on an intimate phone conversation with a best friend. You can tell by the tone of the conversation that they have spent a lot of time on that phone line down across the years. This is not an amateur event—it's spiritual Olympics for them! Anytime our family has special needs I find myself calling on one of them to pray for us. Why? Because I know they have a special relationship with God, and they take prayer seriously.

———

**Prayer is not a lucky charm
for getting what you need;
it is a deepening of relationship
with your best Friend.**

On several occasions I have caught myself starting to worry about a particular matter. The worrying stops almost immediately, however, when I remember that prayer bathes the situation. I do not know how things will turn out or if I will get the answer I am hoping for. Why the peace? Because I know the situation rests in the hands of a God who loves me very much. I can trust Him to do the right thing. Regardless of the outcome, if I am in His care, everything will ultimately fall into place.

Prayer is not so much a lucky charm for getting what you need; it is a deepening of relationship with your best Friend.

Fast Takes

1. Prayer is personal communication with the Father.
2. Jesus taught us almost everything we know about prayer.
3. Prayer is a two-way street with God, like talking on the telephone.
4. Prayer puts our lives in perspective and gives God an opportunity to work in special ways.

Prayer

Thank You, God, for my direct connection to You. What a comfort to know I can call on You at any time and in any circumstance!

Evangelical faith without Christian ethics is a travesty on the gospel.

—V. Raymond Edman

CHAPTER 21

A BILLBOARD FOR GOD

CHRISTIAN ETHICS

Biblical Foundation

"You are to be holy to me because I, the LORD, am holy, and I have set you apart from the nations to be my own" (Lev. 20:26).

"Jesus replied: '"Love the Lord your God with all your heart and with all your soul and with all your mind."' . . . And the second [greatest commandment] is like it: "Love your neighbor as yourself"'" (Matt. 22:37, 39).

Jesus sat on a hill by the Sea of Galilee and preached the Sermon on the Mount. He masterfully reminded His listeners that following God involves more than praying and going to public worship. It also means doing the right things for the right reasons. He said that if you're going to call yourself a Christian, then you should live like a Christian.

The Truth Explained in Everyday Language

Christian ethics deals with the lifestyle choices Christians make as they live their commitment to Jesus Christ at home and in the marketplace. They put feet to doctrine. Paul said we are "a new creation" (2 Cor. 5:17). Our newness of life in Christ makes a difference in the words we use, the jokes we tell, the places we go, the television programs we watch, the way we treat people, the way we spend money, the attitudes we display; the way we act in our home, at work, and at church—and everything else that defines us. Mark Twain once sent a card to a church youth group in Brooklyn with this admonition: "Always do right. This will gratify some people and astonish the rest."[1]

Christian ethics do not come from personal opinion or church rules; they flow from the Bible and carry the authority of God.

Christian ethics do not come from personal opinion or church rules; they flow from the Bible and carry the authority of God. The Bible gives us God's will for conduct. We can accept or reject it, but we cannot change God's mind. Sometimes the Bible offers specific rules for action. It specifically condemns lying, gossiping, stealing, and sex with anyone other than your heterosexual marriage partner. At other times general principles of conduct are deduced from the teachings and life stories of Bible characters. For example, the Bible does not specifically address abortion, but it does address the sanctity of human life.

When we live the Word of God, two things happen. First, Christian character develops. Second, certainty about God's will for moral choices develops. Patterns and habits form that help us feel at home in making godly decisions. Most important, we must look to Jesus Christ as our Example and Model for all moral choices. He's our Big Brother. That's why Hebrews tells us to "fix our eyes on Jesus, the author and perfecter of our faith" (12:2).

After God entered into a contractual relationship with people like Abraham and Moses in the Old Testament, He gave them His law so they could please Him. The Ten Commandments summarize that law (Exod. 20:1-17). They represent a moral contract between God and us. Our commitment to Christ means we agree to follow the Ten Commandments as best we know how. Jesus said, "If anyone loves me, he will obey my teaching" (John 14:23).

Following God involves separation—both separation *from* and separation *to* something. We separate ourselves *from* the mind-set and priorities of the world and separate ourselves *to* the purposes of God. We are reminded in Lev. 19:2, "Be holy because I, the LORD your God, am holy."

Why do the right thing? The Book of Proverbs offers two answers. First, because God commands it, so we reverence Him by obeying His laws—an ethic of obligation (1:7; 15:33). Second, because it makes good sense—an ethic based on good results (11:17). Right living is not an external demand. Rather, it flows naturally from a new internal motivation from God's Spirit. The prophet Ezekiel saw into the New Testament age when he quoted God: "I will give you a new heart and put a new spirit in you; I will remove from you your heart of stone and give you a heart of flesh. And I will put my Spirit in you and move you to follow my decrees and be careful to keep my laws" (36:26-27).

As already noted, salvation is a divine miracle and gift. The same is true for our ability to live Christian ethics. The Bible never assumes we can live by our own resources. We will fall miserably short of the goal. The secret to success is the power of the Holy Spirit. Rom. 8 explains in detail. Note especially verses 5 and 11: "Those who live according to the sinful nature have their minds set on what that nature desires; but those who live in accordance with the Spirit have their minds set on what the Spirit desires. . . . And if the Spirit of him who raised Jesus from the dead is living in you, he who raised Christ from the dead will also give life to your mortal bodies through his Spirit, who lives in you."

**We do not obey God
out of slavish obligation,
but with a child's heart of love.**

We live this way because we love God. We do not obey God out of slavish obligation, but with a child's heart of love. We prefer His ways because we love Him, the same way we try to please a girlfriend, boyfriend, or spouse whom we love very much. No price is too high to show our love. Fidelity to your mate is not a burdensome obligation. The motivation to obey God shines through in Deut. 6:5— "Love the LORD your God with all your heart and with all your soul and with all your strength." Jesus highlighted this in His ministry in Matt. 22:37, 39, quoted at the beginning of this chapter. This becomes the basis of the Golden Rule of Christian ethics: "Do to others what you would have them do to you" (7:12).

With the Bible in our hand and the Spirit of God in our heart, we live the gospel message. God does not leave us on our own in this world to work through the maze of moral possibilities. He stands by our side and directs us every step of the way. He even gives us the power to live it. It's a win-win situation for God and us. We become a living billboard to our world of the life-changing power of God. We are the best proof God has that the Christian message works. As Billy Graham reminds us, "With an acceptance of Christ must go a practice of Christian ethics."[2]

Using the Truth to Enrich Your Life

Most of my friends became Christians because they saw believers model the gospel message. Not irrefutable logic or promise of pie in the sky, but warmth and love won them. The Christian message took on an attractive winsomeness. Believers' smiles and attitudes said, "Something is different with me."

How do we live this life-transforming message before the world? By daily choices. As this chapter began—by the words we use, the jokes we tell, the places we go, the television programs we watch, the way we treat people, the way we spend money, the attitudes we display; the way we act in our home, at work, and at church—and a thousand other choices. Something is fundamentally different about the Christian lifestyle because we operate from a completely different mind-set than that of the world. What's the difference? Our lives are God-centered. The world doesn't always understand *why* we are different, but they certainly notice that we are. We are to be as Phineas F. Bresee puts it, "fountains in the wilderness and rivers in the deserts."[3]

So continue to live close to God, read His Word, be empowered by His Spirit. Then be the best billboard you can be, displaying the life-changing power of the gospel!

Fast Takes

1. Christian ethics put feet to doctrine.
2. Christian ethics come from the Bible and carry the authority of God.
3. Christian ethics are lived by the power of the Holy Spirit and make us a billboard of God's life-changing power.

Prayer

Empower me with Your Spirit and Your Word to represent Your good news to my world today.

LAST THINGS

The truest end of life is to know the life that never ends.

—William Penn

CHAPTER 22

THAT'S ALL, FOLKS

LAST THINGS

Biblical Foundation

"First of all, you must understand that in the last days scoffers will come, scoffing and following their own evil desires. They will say, 'Where is this "coming" he promised? Ever since our fathers died, everything goes on as it has since the beginning of creation'" (2 Pet. 3:3-4).

"As Jesus was sitting on the Mount of Olives, the disciples came to him privately. 'Tell us,' they said, 'when will this happen, and what will be the sign of your coming and of the end of the age?'" (Matt. 24:3).

Jesus preached with the end in mind. He talked about the end of His hearers' personal lives; He talked about the end of His public ministry and life; He talked about the end of the world. Jesus was very definite that our days and the days of our world are numbered. He urged us to make preparation now.

The Truth Explained in Everyday Language

"How's it going to end?" People frequently ask that question every time we experience a great catastrophe in nature, such as a major earthquake, hurricane, or volcano eruption. Every time war breaks out in the Middle East. Every time a breakthrough occurs in global computer technology. Every time a strong dictator makes a bid for greater power. Every time something highly unusual happens in our world, attention turns to this question concerning the end of the world.

The study of last things, or eschatology, as theologians refer to it, is the last important study of Christian faith. More attention has been given to this subject in the past century than in all of church history combined. Why the renewed interest? Perhaps because of the rapid developments in transportation, communication, and technology. Perhaps because of the political unrest in the Middle East and the restoration of Israel as a nation. Perhaps because of the fall of Communism and the massive shifts in world power. Perhaps because of nuclear weapons that have the potential to destroy the entire world a dozen times over. Perhaps because of the rise of power in some third world nations. Perhaps because of worldwide terrorism on airliners and in public buildings. Perhaps because of the social and moral unrest of our world. From a variety of sources comes this renewed interest in the end of the world.

One mark of maturity involves coming to terms with our own mortality.

The study of last things falls into two major categories: my personal end on earth and the end of the world as we know it. My personal end on earth, of course, is physical death. Hebrews reminds us of our mortality: "Man is destined to die once, and after that to face judgment" (9:27). One mark of maturity involves coming to terms with our own mortality. Young people tend to think they are invincible. They do daredevil stunts, taking unnecessary risks. But as time goes on, they become more cautious. As an elderly man once told me, "Death is the black camel that kneels before every door." Paul calls death "the last enemy" for us to conquer (1 Cor. 15:26, 54-56).

Death entered the world through disobedience to God in the Garden of Eden. Why must believers also face death after God forgives them of their sins? Though God loves and forgives us and takes away the eternal consequences of sin, He does not reverse the effects of the choices made in the garden or of our sinful choices before we became a Christian. We accept death as a part of sin's plague.

So regardless of how many more years the world stands or what events happen in the end, our days on earth are numbered. By that I don't mean that God has appointed each of us a certain number of days. Some people teach that when your number comes up, you die. This is not biblical. Life is not like a parking meter that runs out. God is the ultimate Source of all life on earth, and He has providential control of our world. However, He usually chooses to let nature run its course. He does not "take" the life of every one who dies, as so many say. I know numerous people who are bitter and blame God for "killing" their loved ones. God doesn't operate this way. Disease, illness, genetic flaws, accidents, and natural causes play a role in terminating life on earth. No amount of money, power, influence, or spirituality can spare us from our appointment with death. That's one appointment none of us will be late for!

The Bible gives clear testimony that the world as we know it will end someday. This is the second major category in the study of last things. The Bible does not give many details or a time frame. It simply states the certainty of the event. Bible books such as Daniel, Ezekiel, and Revelation offer images of that last day, but we do not have enough understanding to draw a complete picture.

We balance a normal life with a readiness for immediate departure.

A great deal of speculation has been offered across the years about the exact details of the end time. Every generation from Jesus' day until now has pointed to evidences that theirs was the terminal generation. The delay has led many to doubt its certainty. Not a logical conclusion. Delay does not imply error in the biblical declaration. When it happens—and it will—we have the certainty that it will happen just as the Bible said it would. As Jesus put it, "Heaven and earth will pass away, but my words will never pass away" (Matt. 24:35).

Two extremes must be avoided in this regard: (1) building an entire theology or ministry on the end of the world, and (2) totally avoiding the subject. In a parable about the coming of the kingdom of God, Jesus urged us to stay busy with normal life until He returns (Luke 19:13). He also cautioned us to be watchful and ready for the end (Mark 13:33). So we balance a normal life with a readiness for immediate departure.

Much remains uncertain about the details of our death or the end of the world. One thing remains certain about both: they will happen. The Bible intends no doom and gloom but creates a bright hope and reminds us of God's control. Like the elderly woman going through a troublesome time testified in prayer meeting, "I rejoice with my hope in God." In the end, God and His good purposes will triumph. Our sure hope is in Him.

Using the Truth to Enrich Your Life

Speculation about the end of the world abounds. Books, magazine articles, television documentaries, and talk shows offer specific details and dates. Every year brings new dates for the Apocalypse. I saw one today on a grocery store checkout stand magazine.

On several occasions students have stopped by my office to discuss this. I remember Dave's visit the afternoon prior to a predicted "end of the world." He fidgeted with anxiety. He wrung his hands. A look of panic filled his eyes. His world was rocked. "What are we going to do, Prof?" he whined. After calming him down, I discussed the matter in detail. I first asked if he was spiritually prepared to meet the Lord. He was, so I told him he had nothing to worry about. He departed in peace. A few days later he laughed at his panicked reaction. He realized that constant readiness disposes of the need for last-minute preparation.

You've probably had a similar experience. When it happens again, tell your friend not to worry. Be ready to go every day of life, and live normally. Don't let the delay cause loss of hope, though. Remember—delay does not imply error or uncertainty with God. Regardless of whether the world lasts another year, decade, or millennium, we will all die in a relatively short time. Some will die today. With the day of our personal departure uncertain, we must always be ready. Either way, short time or long, our hope is in God.

Fast Takes

1. More attention has been given to the study of last things in this century than in all of church history combined.
2. My life on earth and the existence of the world itself will eventually both come to an end.
3. We must live a normal life but be ready to go at any time.

Prayer

Thank You, God, for certain hope in an uncertain world.

I can almost see the Father saying, "Son, go get my children." And at the midnight cry, we'll be going home. *

—Greg Day and Chuck Day

CHAPTER 23

"I'LL BE BACK"

THE SECOND COMING OF CHRIST

Biblical Foundation

"Keep watch, because you do not know on what day your Lord will come. . . . So you also must be ready, because the Son of Man will come at an hour when you do not expect him" (Matt. 24:42, 44).

"In my Father's house are many rooms; if it were not so, I would have told you. I am going there to prepare a place for you. And if I go and prepare a place for you, I will come back and take you to be with me that you also may be where I am" (John 14:2-3).

Jesus mentioned His return often during His earthly ministry. He wanted His listeners to understand that His ministry involved much more than the present works. The writers of the New Testament also mentioned Jesus' return often in their writings. In fact, the New Testament offers 318 references to the second coming of Christ. This is not an obscure teaching!

The Truth Explained in Everyday Language

Christianity stands alone among the religions of the world in teaching that its Founder will return to earth to claim His followers, bring judgment, and end the world as we know it. The Bible never doubts the

---

*"The Midnight Cry" by Greg Day and Chuck Day. © 1996 Bridgebuilding Music/BMI. All rights reserved. Used by permission of Brentwood-Benson Music Publishing, Inc.

certainty of the event. Much of Jesus' discussion about His return is recorded in Matt. 24 and 25, Mark 13, and Luke 21. Paul discussed it in Phil. 3 and 1 Thess. 4. The two angels who spoke with the disciples on the Mount of Olives following Jesus' ascension back to heaven promised, "This same Jesus, who has been taken from you into heaven, will come back in the same way you have seen him go into heaven" (Acts 1:11).

His return will signal the glorious triumph of God's good plans for the world.

A scriptural composite picture of Christ's return looks something like this. When the Father determines the right time, He will instruct His Son to journey back to earth. The same Jesus who scuffed His sandals over the dusty roads of Israel will personally revisit earth, accompanied by a great host of heavenly angels. He will appear in the eastern sky and will be visible to everyone, not just believers. His return will signal the glorious triumph of God's good plans for the world and will mark the end of time as we know it. "Every knee [will] bow . . . and every tongue confess that Jesus Christ is Lord" (Phil. 2:10-11). Everyone who believed in Him, both those who anticipated His first coming and those who believed in Him after He came to earth, will be honored with Him. The sequence of these events and the Final Judgment are the subjects of the next two chapters.

The second coming of Christ will cause the dead to rise. One of the major debates of the ages has questioned whether only our spirits will be immortal or whether we will have an actual resurrected body. The former view sees no basis for a body, since our current physical one will decay, burn, or be destroyed in some manner. So they say nothing exists to be resurrected. However, Christians need not debate this question.

The Bible clearly teaches a bodily resurrection, though we do not know the nature of our new body. It will be a spiritual body that will never die again or suffer need; we will recognize one another and maintain our personal identity. Christ's resurrection gives us a model and a hope for our own. That is what Paul meant when he said, "Christ has indeed been raised from the dead, the firstfruits of those who have fallen asleep" (1 Cor. 15:20). Because the Father raised Him from the dead and gave Him a resurrected body, we know He will do the same for us (Rom. 8:11).

Who gets resurrected? Only the righteous for eternal life, or both the righteous and the unrighteous? Some people teach that when the unrighteous die, they simply go to sleep and never awaken. Consciousness ceases forever—a convenient way to deal with the problem. The Bible does not teach this. Everyone, righteous and unrighteous alike, will be resurrected for the purpose of judgment. Everyone who has ever lived on the earth will be conscious on that day.

Many of Jesus' teachings and parables, especially those in Matt. 24—25, Mark 13, and Luke 21, focused on His return. As we said in the last chapter, we must live a normal life but be ready to go at any time. The apostle John closes the Book of Revelation with these exciting words of hope: "He who testifies to these things says, 'Yes, I am coming soon.' Amen. Come, Lord Jesus" (22:20).

Using the Truth to Enrich Your Life

Several years ago my wife, Sue, was out of town on business. Brent and I had taken her to the airport to catch her flight, so we knew the exact day and time to meet her return flight. Since we had the house to ourselves for several days, we suspended all household cleaning rules. You can imagine how things looked by the end of the week. A total disaster! We calculated how long it would take us to clean things up, and we put it off as long as possible. When the time came, we quickly went to work and finished the task about five minutes before leaving for the airport. It proved to be a great father-and-son bonding experience, which we still laugh about.

Everyone, righteous and unrighteous alike, will be resurrected for the purpose of judgment.

Our exercise in delinquency wasn't that unusual. In fact, it accurately reflects our human tendency to procrastinate. If Sue had traveled by car and not given us a specific day and time for her return, we couldn't have been so footloose and fancy-free. Jesus knows us better than we know ourselves. That's why He leaves His return date open. If we knew we had another week, month, or year, we might be tempted to delay our readiness. He wants us to be continually ready for Him. His glorious return will be worth all the preparation and anticipation we can give it.

Fast Takes

1. Jesus promised He would return to earth someday.
2. His second coming will signal the resurrection of the dead.
3. The delay in His return does not mean it's not going to happen; it's as certain as all of God's other promises.

Prayer

In all my going and coming, Lord, help me to be ever ready for Your anticipated return.

God does not take away trials or carry us over
them, but strengthens us through them.

—Edward B. Pusey

CHAPTER 24

WHAT'S AHEAD?

TRIBULATION AND MILLENNIAL VIEWS

Biblical Foundation

*"Then there will be great distress, unequaled from the begin-
ning of the world until now—and never to be equaled again. If
those days had not been cut short, no one would survive, but for the
sake of the elect those days will be shortened"* (Matt. 24:21-22).

*"Blessed and holy are those who have part in the first resurrec-
tion. The second death has no power over them, but they will be
priests of God and of Christ and will reign with him for a thousand
years"* (Rev. 20:6).

Jesus talked during His earthly ministry about the Tribulation. He
did not want His followers to be surprised by it. Some of His predic-
tions came true when the Romans invaded Jerusalem in A.D. 70. Others will not come to pass until the end of time. Either way, He wanted
us to be prepared for the day of trouble when it arrives. Jesus did not
say anything specifically about a thousand-year reign on earth, so we
cannot know anything definite about that.

The Truth Explained in Everyday Language

My dad always said hindsight is clearer than foresight. That is
certainly the case when discussing the sequence of events for the end
of time. We'll have 20/20 vision about it 10,000 years from now. The
Bible gives us a variety of puzzle pieces but does not put them together for us. Perhaps God intended to give us hope and the assurance
that we are predestined for final victory but not to worry us with all

the details. Thus, we should not give too much attention to all the end-time charts, graphs, and books flooding the market. They offer human speculation—nothing more. I am confident that only when all of the events prophesied in Scripture take place will we realize what God had in mind all along. But until then we must exercise caution in our speculation.

I am confident that only when all of the events prophesied in Scripture take place will we realize what God had in mind all along.

Unfortunately, some Christians have elevated their particular end-time speculations to dogmatic tests of faith. They require you to see things their way before they will accept you as a Christian. We must remember that many believers who very deeply love God and His Word interpret end-time passages differently. End-time formulas are not essentials of the faith. Therefore, we must remain charitable to positions other than our own. Only God knows how events will occur in the end.

Information about the Tribulation comes primarily from Matt. 24, Mark 13, Luke 21, and Rev. 13—14. Christians have suffered tribulation for the cause of Christ for nearly 2,000 years. Jesus told His disciples, "In this world you will have trouble. But take heart! I have overcome the world" (John 16:33). Church history records persecution and martyrdom from New Testament days until now. In fact, more people have died for the cause of Christ in the 20th century than in all other centuries combined.

The Tribulation at the end of time will persecute Christians much as they suffer now, only more intensely. The following are various ways people interpret the Great Tribulation. All agree that it refers to a period at the very end of time. Disagreement comes over whether believers suffer through it or not.

1. *Pretribulation view.* God will take all believers out of the world before the Tribulation begins, thus allowing them to avoid the pain and suffering of the end-time events. This unannounced departure is called "the Rapture" and may happen at any moment, signaling the beginning of the end.
2. *Midtribulation view.* God will take all believers out of the world sometime during the Tribulation, before things get really bad. This will allow them to avoid the worst pain and suffering at the end.

3. *Postribulation view.* God will leave all believers on the earth during the Tribulation and allow them to experience persecution just as they have in centuries past. The Antichrist will try to defeat God's saints and drive His presence from the earth. However, God will protect His children throughout the Tribulation and especially when He pours His wrath out at the end of the period (Rev. 13:7; 16:2).

The Bible also mentions the concept of the millennium. The idea begins with Old Testament visions of a reign of the Messiah, bringing righteousness and holiness throughout the earth (Dan. 7). It continues in the New Testament with Jesus' discussions of the messianic Kingdom and the rule of His followers in it (Matt. 19:28). Jesus did not, however, specify a thousand-year period of time on earth prior to His heavenly reign.

**We must not get lost
in the various arguments
but keep God's purpose in mind
for telling us what little we know
about it—to give us hope and
the assurance that His followers
are predestined for victory in the end.**

The concept of a thousand-year period comes from Rev. 20:1-6. The number 1,000 comes from adding the biblically special numbers 3 and 7 together and cubing the sum, thus making 1,000 a reference to absolute perfection. Those who interpret the passage literally say Christ will have a millennial rule on earth with His saints prior to the end of the world and the Final Judgment. Those who interpret the passage figuratively, as they do most of the Book of Revelation, either see it as a reference to the growth of the kingdom of God through the Church from Bible times until the end of the world or see it as the reign of Christ eternally in heaven.

The following represent the central millennial views:

1. *Premillennial view.* This is a literal interpretation that following the Great Tribulation and prior to the Final Judgment, Christ will rule on the earth.

2. *Postmillennial view.* We are now part of the millennium because the kingdom of God is a present reality on earth through the Church. The gospel will spread to all nations of the world; then the Great Tribulation will come. Christ will return to earth, bringing judgment with assignments to heaven or hell.

3. *Amillennial view.* The thousand-year period is symbolic of the Church age. Christ will reign over all things in His heavenly rule after the Final Judgment. It agrees with the postmillennial view in many ways.

Remember—all these positions use Scripture to validate their stand and answer objections. None are flawless. So don't judge those who do not interpret things as you currently see them. I say "currently," because even the best Bible scholars often change their positions over time and introduce "new and improved" ideas. We must not get lost in the various arguments but keep God's purpose in mind for telling us what little we know about it—to give us hope and the assurance that His followers are predestined for victory in the end.

Using the Truth to Enrich Your Life

When I was in the eighth grade, our science teacher told us a science project would be required the following year. All our projects would be displayed in the school gym. He didn't give us too many details; he simply advised us to think about it and give it our best effort. The winning project in each category would compete in a district contest. The winners at the district level would go on to compete in a state contest. Students who made it to the state level would get an all-expenses-paid trip to the state capital for three days, which meant three days away from school.

I didn't know much about it, but I determined right then that I wanted to win that prize the next year. I worked hard for several months. My mom helped me research in the library, and my dad helped me build my light experiment. I won both the local and district contests and got to compete at the state level. It was an experience that I treasure to this day.

Why did I work so hard for that prize? Because our science teacher told us just enough information to whet our appetites but not enough to satisfy our curiosities. We were driven by the mystery and the goal of winning.

That may be what God had in mind when He gave us a few glimpses of the end of the age. We don't know much about it; we wish we knew more. All we know for sure is that God and those on His side win in the end. The reward defies descriptions. We are driven by the mystery and the goal of winning. Let's determine to make it there together! It will be worth all the effort we can give it!

Fast Takes

1. God whets our appetite with a few glimpses about the end time to give us hope and the assurance of victory.

2. The world will experience a great tribulation at the end of time.
3. Christ will one day reign over all creation.

Prayer

Lord, I don't know too much about what's going to happen at the end of time, but I know You are in charge, and so I place my confidence in You.

My great concern is not whether God is on our side; my great concern is to be on God's side.
—Abraham Lincoln

CHAPTER 25

FINAL DECISION

JUDGMENT DAY

Biblical Foundation

"Man is destined to die once, and after that to face judgment" (Heb. 9:27).

"For he [God] has set a day when he will judge the world with justice by the man [Jesus Christ] he has appointed. He has given proof of this to all men by raising him from the dead" (Acts 17:31).

Jesus spoke with certainty that Judgment Day will eventually come. He often referenced it in His teachings. He never seemed to be overly troubled by the apparent victory of His enemies. Our Lord knew such victories were temporary. Enemies may have won an occasional battle against God, but He wins the war in the end.

The Truth Explained in Everyday Language

When I was a child, I sometimes complained to my grandmother about the injustice of a schoolyard bully. She would always shake her little index finger at me and reply, "Don't you worry about it. He'll get his in the end." I didn't find her answer very consoling. I wanted to see justice—*now*. As I grew older, Mom would say, "Remember, 'Vengeance is mine; I will repay, saith the Lord'" (Rom. 12:19, KJV). I didn't find her advice very helpful either. Then when I became a father, I found myself saying the same things to my son.

"Life's not fair, Dad."

"Who said life's fair, Son? Remember—God doesn't balance His books every Friday."

I don't think my words helped Brent any more than Mom's words helped me at the time.

God may not balance
His books every Friday,
but He *does* balance them.

It's true: God may not balance His books every Friday, but He *does* balance them. As Aunt Stella used to say, "Though the mills of God grind slowly, yet they grind exceeding small."[1] He will set everything in life straight one day. The Bible refers to that time as "the day of the Lord" (Mal. 4:5; 1 Cor. 5:5; 2 Cor. 1:14; 1 Thess. 5:2; 2 Pet. 3:10.)

We're not too sure about end-time details, but the Bible explicitly describes what will happen on this day. Following the second coming of Christ and the bodily resurrection of everyone who has ever lived on earth, Christ will sit in the seat of judgment. Everyone, both righteous and unrighteous, will appear before Him for final judgment. Those who had faith in Christ as Savior will stand on His right, and those who rejected Him on His left. Satan and the demons will also receive their final judgment on that day.

Everyone present will take a turn to step forward when his or her name is called. Something like a large video screen will display our life with words, actions, thoughts, motives, and secrets for all to see. The truth about everything will be known on that day. This may have been the reference of Jesus when He said, "There is nothing concealed that will not be disclosed, or hidden that will not be made known. What you have said in the dark will be heard in the daylight, and what you have whispered in the ear in the inner rooms will be proclaimed from the roofs" (Luke 12:2-3). Christians have a special advantage when they stand for judgment. Everything we have asked God to forgive us of will be erased, like the 18 minutes from United States President Richard Nixon's famous telephone tapes. It cannot condemn us. That's another marvelous benefit of our salvation.

Our salvation will be determined by simply trusting Christ; however, that's not all that will be decided. Our works will also be judged, not as merit to win God's favor, but as fruit or evidence of our commitment to Christ. Jesus said, "If you love me, you will obey what I command" (John 14:15). The measuring stick for judgment will not be a particular number of tasks accomplished, goals reached, dollars given, prayers prayed, or any other material data. The standard of judgment will be our faithfulness to God's revealed will for our lives. In other words, did we do what God asked us to do? Were we faithful to our assignment? As Mother Teresa said, "I do not pray for success. I ask for faithfulness."[2]

Why judge our works? To determine degrees of reward and punishment. Speculation abounds about how God gives degrees of reward and punishment. Some, like Dante in his literary work *The Inferno*, imagine heaven and hell with layers, but that's not biblical. Others see heaven with big mansions for great rewards and small huts for small ones, or hell with big flames for great punishment and little flames for small ones.

"I do not pray for success.
I ask for faithfulness."
—Mother Teresa

Could we enjoy heaven as God says we will if many of our friends receive greater rewards than we do? That's a good question. Obviously, no one knows the answer. I personally imagine degrees of reward as our ability to comprehend and appreciate the beauty and joy of heaven. Let me explain. I'm not very handy in the kitchen; actually, I'm a disaster. My last culinary attempt got me banned from the stove until further notice. Sue, on the other hand, is a master cook, an artist of fine cuisine. When we eat out together, I can tell you if I like something or not, but I don't know why. Either it tastes good to me, or it doesn't. Sue can taste specific ingredients in foods and how much of each was used. She has a far superior ability to discern tastes than I do. In heaven, those with the greatest reward will have the greatest comprehension and appreciation for what they are experiencing. Degrees of punishment will have a similar basis. It's not a perfect analogy, but it helps me.

One thing is certain about Judgment Day: all decisions are final. No appeals to a heavenly Supreme Court. No chance for declaring a mistrial. No retrials. Jesus Christ will have all the facts; no information will be missing. He will have perfect judgment with which to judge; His perspective will not be clouded or skewed. No one will resist, and no one will rebel against His judgment. When He declares His verdict, all reality will accept it.

Using the Truth to Enrich Your Life

We all experience injustice at some point in life. Schoolyard bullies. Workplace lies. Prejudice. Random acts of violence. Terrorism. Dishonest business deals. Misunderstanding friends. The list is endless. We wish we could go back and make things right, but we can't. We have to learn to move on and live with the injustice.

Christians have the consolation that God sees and hears everything, and He keeps accurate records. He also doesn't forget. We sometimes get frustrated when we see His plans and purposes defeated. Sometimes we even feel as though evil may triumph; it won't. No, God remains in control, and He will have His final say on His day. That's why the Bible calls it "the day of the Lord." God is like a schoolteacher who sits quietly, listening to everybody's side of the story. He is taking it all in right now. He is even giving us a chance to repent and amend our ways so He can erase the negative part of our record. But one day He will say, "Enough." And that will be it!

Fast Takes

1. God doesn't balance His books as often as we would like, but He *does* balance them.
2. Every person who has ever lived will stand before Christ and give a life account.
3. Good works do not earn salvation, but they increase our enjoyment of heaven.
4. All Judgment Day decisions will be final.

Prayer

Lord, help me to live this day with an awareness that You see everything and will someday make all things right.

If I find in myself a desire which no experience in this world can satisfy, the most probable explanation is that I was made for another world.

—C. S. Lewis

CHAPTER 26

HOME AT LAST

HEAVEN

Biblical Foundation

> "The Lord himself will come down from heaven, with a loud command, with the voice of the archangel and with the trumpet call of God, and the dead in Christ will rise first. After that, we who are still alive and are left will be caught up together with them in the clouds to meet the Lord in the air. And so we will be with the Lord forever" (1 Thess. 4:16-17).

> "Then I saw a new heaven and a new earth, for the first heaven and the first earth had passed away, and there was no longer any sea. I saw the Holy City, the new Jerusalem, coming down out of heaven from God, prepared as a bride beautifully dressed for her husband" (Rev. 21:1-2).

Jesus talked about heaven from a personal perspective. He had firsthand knowledge about what we can expect. He talked as matter-of-factly about heaven as if it were around the corner or down the street. He took the fear and mystery away and replaced it with beautiful and inviting images. His best image pictures a loving Father standing at the door awaiting our arrival.

The Truth Explained in Everyday Language

C. S. Lewis said it best: "I was made for another world." All the good things this world offers are never enough. From deep within our souls comes a longing for our heavenly home. As settled as we get here with an address and a name in the phone book, we still feel like pilgrims passing through. We are homesick for our final resting-place. Paul reminded us, "Our citizenship is in heaven" (Phil. 3:20). We are resident aliens, keeping a light touch on earthly things.

This mind-set does not mean we withdraw from normal earthly life; we are actively involved in our world as Christ's hands and feet, ministering to the needs of those around us. Rather, this mind-set keeps life in perspective for us. It helps us sift the important from the trivial, the eternal from the mundane. It reminds us that this life is not the whole story. We are preparing our souls for a much higher purpose and a much better place. Life here is judged by its relationship to life there.

Heaven is the place where the nature of God shines forth.

What does the Bible mean by the word "heaven"? Sometimes it means the entire universe—as the Bible begins, "In the beginning God created the heavens and the earth" (Gen. 1:1). Sometimes it refers to God. As the prodigal son resolved, "I will set out and go back to my father and say to him: 'Father, I have sinned against heaven and against you'" (Luke 15:18). Sometimes it refers to the spiritual realm of life, as Paul referred to with "the rulers and authorities in the heavenly realms" (Eph. 3:10). But most often the Bible uses the word "heaven" to refer to the dwelling place of God and His followers. As the Lord's Prayer begins, "Our Father in heaven" (Matt. 6:9).

We sing many songs about heaven. We read many Bible passages about it. We think about it often when friends and loved ones die. So what is heaven going to be like? That's a difficult question to answer, because our language fails to capture it in words; heaven defies description. The loftiest and grandest words we use to picture it give us a dim black-and-white snapshot rather than a full-color video. But what little we can say about heaven makes it very inviting.

Let's start with the best news. God dwells there eternally. In fact, God's presence defines heaven. Yet it's not just one specific plot of ground with one mailbox, so to speak. Since God occupies all creation and beyond, then heaven can be defined as wherever He dwells. You say, "But God's presence is on earth right now, and earth isn't heaven." Why not? Because of the effects and damage of sin and the presence of evil people. That, then, must also enter our picture. Heaven means the absence of all evil and all of the effects and damage of sin.

God's presence is fully felt and His will fully followed. He is the Crown Jewel of everything. So heaven is both a place and a state. It is a place where we have bodily form and live a life of activity, and it is a state in which God's presence dwells unhindered.

The Bible describes heaven with rare and expensive objects: gold, silver, jasper, and pearls. The gates of pearl and streets of gold (Rev. 21:21) mean that the most expensive things of earth are as common as dirt in heaven. The standard of life there cannot be compared with earthly standards. In the last 100 years or so, Christians have gotten sidetracked with materialistic thoughts of big white mansions on spaciously manicured lots, and long, sleek luxury cars. This cheapens the biblical picture because it appeals to the materialistic appetite of human nature. We shouldn't want to go to heaven to cash in on God's lottery! We long for heaven to be with Him in His perfect home.

Heaven is the place where the nature of God shines forth. Here we see an unhindered display of His holiness, love, righteousness, truth, justice, grace, joy, and mercy. The river of all life flows from God himself through the middle of heaven, sustaining life for all. We will enter heaven with our newly resurrected body, so we will recognize people and renew old acquaintances. Fellowship with one another will be at a deeper level than it is now. We will receive a clear perspective on everything.

**We will live in a
constant state of
completion, satisfaction,
and fulfillment
because we enjoy the
unhindered presence of God.**

What will be missing from heaven? All of God's enemies and all influences of evil. Everything unclean and everything that destroys will be gone too. No tears, mourning, pain, need, or death will enter there. Neither will there be misunderstanding or haunting thoughts of past failures. We do not know how God will accomplish the renewal of our minds, but the failures of this life will be removed, along with the painful memories of friends and family who rejected Christ. God will make everything new (Rev. 21:5).

What will we do in heaven? A variety of things. We will worship and praise God as a constant part of life. We will be involved in the Lord's work in some way as the angels are now, though we don't understand that yet. We will fellowship with one another. We will study and learn as we search the depths of God's knowledge and understanding. We will be able to fulfill the imaginations of our heart, which were often thwarted in this life. We will rest from the struggle against sin, the flesh, and the devil. Even our activity can be classified as rest because it will be stress-free. We will live in a constant state of completion, satisfaction, and fulfillment—not because we are living in luxury, but because we enjoy the unhindered presence of God.

Using the Truth to Enrich Your Life

Life on earth is full of clues about heaven. Here's one. Scientists have discovered that the human brain is the most complex computer ever known. The artificial intelligence of our current class of supercomputers does not compare with that of our brains. A series of computers matching one brain's ability would fill a large room. Yet the human brain is so small and compact.

We grasp that mystery fairly well. Now here's the clincher: all the functions that our human brain performs in operating our body, creating conversation, organizing our work, storing our memories, giving us an imagination, and accessing the spiritual side of life all put together, use only about 2 percent of its capacity! Can you imagine that? God loaded incredibly more computer power in our brain than we could ever need in this life. Why do you suppose He went so far overboard? I think it might be another of His subtle clues to remind us that this life is not all there is. When we get to heaven, maybe we can access some of that 98 percent of unused brain power. Who knows? He may even give us a bigger model that will further blow our circuits!

Remember: everything we have said in this chapter doesn't even scratch the surface of the wonder and beauty of heaven. It will be better than we ever imagined it.

Fast Takes

1. Thoughts of heaven do not take us from our ministry assignments on earth, but they do help us keep life in perspective.
2. The presence of God makes heaven the wonderful place that it is.
3. The most expensive things of earth are as common as dirt in heaven.
4. Heaven will be a place of stress-free completion, satisfaction, and fulfillment.

Prayer

I live this day, O Lord of life, with the excited awareness that someday I will live with You forever.

All hope abandon, ye who enter here!

—Dante

CHAPTER 27

FOREVER LOST

HELL

Biblical Foundation

> *"As the weeds are pulled up and burned in the fire, so it will be at the end of the age. The Son of Man will send out his angels, and they will weed out of his kingdom everything that causes sin and all who do evil. They will throw them into the fiery furnace, where there will be weeping and gnashing of teeth" (Matt. 13:40-42).*

> *"Then death and Hades were thrown into the lake of fire. The lake of fire is the second death. If anyone's name was not found written in the book of life, he was thrown into the lake of fire" (Rev. 20:14-15).*

Jesus invited sinners to God and held out a loving hand of healing and hope—a very positive ministry. But this did not prevent His discussion of hell. His message was a double-edged sword. He offered salvation and hope, but that offer required a choice. People could either accept His offer or reject it. If they rejected, they would have to live with the consequences of their choice.

The Truth Explained in Everyday Language

The discussion of hell has fallen on hard times in recent years. It is no longer politically correct to talk about a place of eternal punishment. Ministers have actually been sued and charged with creating mental distress for preaching on the subject. But regardless of how culturally taboo the subject becomes, it remains a clear warning of Scripture.

Talk of hell offends for a number of reasons. For one thing, people argue that a God of love cannot also be a God of judgment. Others contend no place could be that bad for all eternity. Still others do not take the Bible literally in its language on hell; they believe hell means living with the consequences of bad choices or annihilation at death. Some even go so far as to say the discussion on hell is a scare tactic to get people to live better, contending that regardless of how they live, God will take everyone to heaven in the end.

Let's examine these arguments. The first addresses the judgment of God. God's judgment doesn't impose a sentence on people; it honors their will to reject Him. He sends no one to hell against their will; they choose it. C. S. Lewis says that if we refuse to say, "Thy will be done," God says to us, "Thy will be done."[1] Jesus said these people prefer darkness to light because their deeds are evil (John 3:19). How would they like being taken to heaven against their will? They would be miserable in a place that focuses on the honor and worship of God—something they refuse to do.

Hell's doors lock
from the inside.

The second argument questions the eternal nature of hell. The people who go there have had ample opportunity in this life to surrender their wills to God's will. They choose to remain rebellious against Him. So hell's doors lock from the inside. God simply stays away from this place where He is not welcome. Since He is eternal, then He can stay away from hell for eternity. The biblical language speaks in terms of *eternal* death, *eternal* fire, and *eternal* punishment. It offers no hope for a termination date. As my pastor said, "There is no redemption from hell."

Some hold out hope for "the eternal restoration of all things." They argue that since hell is created, it must end someday, because all created things will eventually end. The idea comes from Paul's discussion in Eph. 1:9-10, in which he says God will "bring all things in heaven and on earth together under one head, even Christ" (v. 10). Paul's reference is to God restoring His creation to the way it was prior to the Fall, not to blessing rebellious people with heavenly reward.

The third argument questions the literal nature of hell. The Bible speaks in very literal terms. Jesus did everything He could to describe hell in common language that people could understand—literal language (see Matt. 5:22, 29). He talked about the city dump of Jerusalem in the valley of Hinnom, a place where fires burned day and night. He talked in the story of the rich man and Lazarus about a literal place with real thirst, torment, agony, fire, and haunting memories of bad choices made on earth (Luke 16:19-31).

The Bible never even hints that hell is figurative language for consequences of bad choices. Such ideas come from human reason trying to dismiss biblical truth. We have no basis to interpret Jesus' descriptions of hell as figurative.

What does the Bible say about hell? It calls it a real place and a state of mind just as heaven is both a place and a state. The unrighteous will be resurrected for judgment along with the righteous. So hell will be more than a mental state. Individuals will suffer bodily. They will also suffer loneliness, hopelessness, the mental torment of past decisions, and the way they mistreated people and God. Time becomes perpetual. Jesus described it as a place "where 'their worm does not die, and the fire is not quenched'" (Mark 9:48).

God's presence defines heaven; His absence defines hell.

All these descriptions of hell fail to capture its worst feature—the absence of God. His presence defines heaven; His absence defines hell. We live with God's blessings all around us. Therefore, we cannot possibly imagine life without Him. That's why no words properly capture hell. God honors our will to accept Christ while we live on earth, but He reserves the right to lock that decision in at the point of death. No second chances; no changing our minds.

God governs the universe righteously. He assumes responsibility for defending the virtues that come from His nature, like truth, honesty, righteousness, holiness, and justice. Judgment Day will set the record straight on all these matters. After God passes judgment on sin and rebellion, He must follow through with the deserved punishment. Otherwise, moral order will be lost. Imagine that the worst sinner who ever lived was greeted at heaven's gates with, "Come on in. It doesn't matter how you lived and that you never accepted Christ. Everyone goes to heaven!" God could not do that. People must receive the consequences of their actions. It's just that simple.

Using the Truth to Enrich Your Life

We live in a day when people do not want to assume responsibility for their behavior. They want to do whatever they want to do, then walk away from responsibility. They blame anyone and everyone for their choices: society, dysfunctional family, genetics. Excuses never cease. They say in effect, "I'm a victim and can't be held responsible for my behavior." I see this attitude all the time. You probably do as well. It's a national epidemic.

Fortunately, God doesn't accept this excuse. He gives us the free-

dom of personal choice and then holds us responsible for the consequences of those choices. As Abraham Lincoln said, "You can fool all
the people some of the time." But we can't fool God. He keeps accurate records, and He judges with perfect judgment. He will make no
mistake in holding us responsible for our actions.

That's why it's important for us to ask God to give us what the
old-timers called "Judgment Day honesty" as we contemplate our daily choices. We have an incredible ability to rationalize our behavior
and defend ourselves. Such rationalization does not work with God.
We must ask Him to help us to see matters as He sees them.

Notice that this application focuses on "us," and not "them"—the
Christians, and not the sinners. Discussions of hell easily focus on
anyone but ourselves. We must not use this information to pass judgment on others; let God do that. We must concentrate on sharing the
Good News, living righteous lives, and trusting God for our salvation.
Remember: God's judgment will begin with us, so we must be prepared (1 Pet. 4:17).

Fast Takes

1. The subject of hell is no longer politically correct, but it remains a clear message of Scripture.
2. Hell results from God honoring sinners' request to reject Him.
3. Hell can be eternal, because God is eternal.

Prayer

Help me, Father, to live today with Judgment Day honesty.

He who provides for this life, but takes no care for eternity, is wise for a moment, but a fool forever.

—Tillotson

CHAPTER 28

TIME EVERMORE

ETERNITY

Biblical Foundation

"He has made everything beautiful in its time. He has also set eternity in the hearts of men; yet they cannot fathom what God has done from beginning to end" (Eccles. 3:11).

"I tell you the truth, whoever hears my word and believes him who sent me has eternal life and will not be condemned; he has crossed over from death to life" (John 5:24).

Jesus spoke often of eternal life. That was the focus of His discussion with Nicodemus in John 3. He gave us a clear picture of life after this life on earth. For those who accept Him as Savior there will be life evermore. We will share fellowship with Him and with one another for all eternity.

The Truth Explained in Everyday Language

Our culture is very time-conscious. We wear watches and have clocks in our homes, offices, cars, and public buildings. In fact, a timepiece is almost always within sight. We expect events to start and end on time. We want planes and trains to operate on schedule. We don't like to be kept waiting. We try to fill every waking moment with activity. Time is a commodity, so we attempt to make the most of it.

The Bible uses the word "time" in two different ways: (1) as simple duration with one minute passing another and (2) as a special moment of opportunity. The first simply records two o'clock turning into three o'clock and so forth through the day. The second occurs when waiting at the airport for a loved one to arrive or by the telephone for a medical report. The minutes hang like hours. The minutes speed by, however, when we participate with a loved one in a special activity, like taking a walk through the park with our mate or playing games with our child. We wish we could stop the clock and savor the moment. As Cesare Pavese said, "We do not remember days—we remember moments."[1]

The Bible usually speaks of time in terms of the second usage. It's not the passing of moments that make up life, but the talks with friends, the walks through nature, the meaningful seasons of prayer, the overwhelming sense of God's presence. One experience or event after another with friends, loved ones, and God make up the fabric of our lives. Our memories help us celebrate the moments of life. This biblical usage of time sheds light on an understanding of eternity.

This life that lasts for eternity comes to us as God's gift.

The Bible speaks often of eternity, not as the absence of time, like stopping the clock, but as the endless succession of time. Eternity does not start when earthly time ends—it stretches earthly time out for ever and ever. However, it's more than one minute passing another endlessly, as with the first use of the word "time." That could get monotonous and boring. Eternity contains a perpetual succession of special moments for heavenly residents. For God resides there, too, bringing deep and rich meaning to each moment. Our schedules will be filled with fulfilling fellowship and experiences with God, friends, and loved ones. We will say to ourselves, "I wish this could last forever"— and it will!

Time is a real thing, not just a construction of the mind. It comes from God just as our life comes from Him. He, in fact, gives time meaning. "'I am the Alpha and the Omega,' says the Lord God, 'who is, and who was, and who is to come, the Almighty'" (Rev. 1:8). He has been, is, and will be present at every period of time.

"Eternal life" appears 42 times in the New Testament. Jesus used it often. It refers both to duration of time and quality of life. According to the Bible, eternal life does not begin the moment we die; it begins the moment we accept Jesus Christ as personal Savior. Jesus said, "Whoever believes in the Son has eternal life" (John 3:36). Believing in Jesus means putting your simple trust in Him alone for salvation. It also means turning your back on the world's values (Luke 18:28-30). It involves self-sacrifice (John 12:25) and service to God (4:35-36). Life centers on spiritual matters and staying in tune with the Spirit of God (Gal. 6:8). As my childhood pastor used to say, "Eternal life gives us a little heaven down here to go to heaven in." Believers in this life already have endless duration of life and meaningful quality of life.

When you put the concepts of eternity and eternal life together, a picture emerges. This life that lasts for eternity comes to us as God's gift. We do not earn or deserve it. God's eternal life has no beginning or end; our eternal life has a beginning when we accept Christ, but it has no end.

Eternal life in heaven completes our salvation, which begins the moment we believe in Jesus as Savior. It involves living a life filled with righteousness, holiness, love, joy, goodness, and all the other attributes of God that He shares with us. We will grow in these qualities unhindered by Satan and the forces of evil for all eternity. The focus of heaven's life will be spiritual rather than physical, and quality rather than quantity. The spiritual quality of life will be so great that we will never get bored or tired of it. And finally, God will be the focal point of eternal life. The life that comes from Him will find its fulfillment in praising and worshiping Him.

Some people err in their analysis of eternal life. They say that we will grow and develop in heaven until we become gods. Not so. While we will have an endless potential for growth and development, we will always remain creatures. God will remain Creator. Thus, there will always be a qualitative difference between Creator and creature. Dogs can't become cats; apples can't become oranges; people can't become gods.

When you put the concepts of eternity and eternal death together, the opposite picture emerges. Eternal death will also have an endless duration. The absence of God's presence brings the absence of life, fulfillment, meaning, quality, and all the other good things taking place in heaven. Remember—God does not vindictively send people into eternal death against their wills. They freely choose it by refusing to accept God's forgiveness and the gift of eternal life. Jesus said, "As for the person who hears my words but does not keep them, I do not judge him. For I did not come to judge the world, but to save it. There is a judge for the one who rejects me and does not accept my words; that very word which I spoke will condemn him at the last day" (John 12:47-48).

Using the Truth to Enrich Your Life

I often hear the phrase "All good things must come to an end." That's the nature of good things in this life. So we become conditioned to accept the passing of favorable circumstances. I enjoy spending time with my wife, doing things with her, enjoying her company. It might be sitting on the couch listening to music, eating a meal in a restaurant, walking along the beach while on vacation. It becomes a high moment of life. I find myself wanting to stop the clock; I don't want the moment to end. But it does, and life goes on.

———

God's presence will be as near as the air we breathe here on earth.

Eternity won't just be an extended period of existence as it is on earth. Who needs that much hassle? The quality of life will rise to a different level. It will be like the high moments of this life. We get a glimpse of that thought after a wonderful worship service when people linger around the church. They want to savor the moment and take it with them. The atmosphere of heaven will be just like that; we will take it with us wherever we go. God's presence will be as near as the air we breathe here on earth.

Words are such poor containers for heavenly thoughts. God has so much more planned for us than we can possibly imagine. Stay true to Him, and He will reward you—forever!

Fast Takes

1. Eternity is not the absence of time; it is the endless succession of it.
2. Eternal life begins not when we die but when we believe in Christ as Savior.
3. The spiritual quality of life will be so great in heaven that we will never get bored or tired of it; it will be endless fulfillment with God.

Prayer

Thank You, God, for daily fellowship with You, which will last for all eternity.

CONCLUSION

SEE YOU LATER

This concludes our coffee shop chat about the faith. I hope you haven't been drinking coffee the whole time you read this book! I do hope, however, that several things happened as you read.

1. I hope you enjoyed it. Of course, I doubt you'd still be reading it if you didn't—unless you're one of those persons who turns to the last chapter to see how a book ends!

2. I hope you found ways to become more like Christ. That is always the goal of learning more about our faith. Jesus came to earth to give us a worthy example.

3. I hope you gained a new appreciation for theology. Theology is more than a set of doctrines to believe or ethical practices to follow. It is a story—a story about an incredible love affair, God's love affair with us. So theology shouldn't scare you off or turn you off. It's our way of learning more about the God who loves us so much.

4. I hope you gained a new perspective on God's love for you. His love never ceases to amaze me. I have spent my entire adult life studying it. I talk about it in class every day. I have hundreds of examples and illustrations about it. Yet when I stop and contemplate it, it amazes me as though I am hearing about it for the first time. It is perpetually fresh.

5. I hope you gained a hunger to learn more about your faith. Studying theology both satisfies your hunger and creates an appetite to learn more. This book only touches the edges of our faith with a thumbnail sketch. Most readers won't want to go out and get a degree in theology. But I hope you will do further reading in some of the areas that interest you. Ask your pastor for advice on books to further your study in those areas.

6. I hope you see the bigger picture of God's plan for us. Jesus' entire ministry as well as the entire biblical message center on God's desire to restore fellowship with fallen humanity. He comes to us in a thousand different ways and offers us a return ticket to himself. Jesus pictured our Father as the prodigal son's dad—standing at the living room window awaiting our return. The porch light is on all night.

7. I hope you learned that you don't master your faith; it masters you. By that I simply mean this: you will never fully understand or contain it in your mind. You will never reach the point in your learning in which you say, "Now I know it all; I can move on to another subject." Your faith works like yeast placed in a lump of dough. It takes over the lump, grows, and changes it into something better than it was before. The yeast masters the dough. After a lifetime of study, I still hunger to know more about my faith, to be mastered by it.

8. I hope you saw the personal and practical side of theology. I told you a lot of personal stories, but you could easily replace them with yours. Think of ways to make each chapter work personally in your life. Theology works practically. It helps us in our church responsibilities; it helps us at work; it helps us raise our kids. Theology translates into daily living and enriches the journey.

9. I hope you learned that Christianity is not a religion. Religion is defined as the human search for God. The world faiths are religions. I will never forget the day Sue and I stood by a shrine in Kyoto, Japan, and watched a poor little woman cry her heart out to a waterfall. She came to pray for her husband's healing by reaching out to the waterfall for help. Christianity, on the other hand, is God's search for us. "We love him, because he first loved [and sought] us" (1 John 4:19, KJV).

10. I hope you gained new information for sharing your faith with non-Christian friends and coworkers. God charges us with the responsibility of being salt, light, and yeast in our world. We do that when we live righteous lives and when we tell others about the good news of Jesus Christ. Your friends have serious questions that push into their waking thoughts and sleepless nights. Help them find answers in God's Word.

11. I hope you have been encouraged to pass your faith on to the next generation. If you have children or grandchildren, you have the privilege of sharing this incredible Good News with them. If you have no children, involve yourself in youthful lives at church or in your community. Find ways to bring your faith alive to them; share the hope that energizes you.

12. I hope you learned that our faith is a never-ending story. We learn all we can and grow all we can in this life, but this life is only the beginning. We will learn about the infinite love and wisdom of God for all eternity. We will also grow and develop while ages roll. The day our faith becomes sight, we will just turn the page to a new chapter in this never-ending story!

The bottom line is this: theology changes life for the better. It makes us more Christlike and eventually leads us to heaven.

Let me tell you about a young man named Kurt. Last year he dropped into a revival service at our church. To this day he does not know why he came. He said he would have laughed at you if you had told him that morning that he would be in a church service that evening. Religion had never been a part of his life; he had never attended church and never read a Bible. Nevertheless, he miraculously found himself at our revival service. The Spirit of God gripped his heart deeply that night, and he accepted the invitation to invite Christ into his life.

Kurt has been in my Sunday School class almost every week for the past two years. He reads his Bible and asks a lot of questions about his faith. He has an unquenchable curiosity. He has grown spiritually by leaps and bounds. I asked him last week why he had stuck with his decision and remained a Christian. He responded, "Up to that point, I had tried everything I could find to meet the need of my heart. Nothing satisfied for very long. Each thing I tried left me empty and searching. When I tried Christ, I had reached the end of myself. He satisfied the need of my life as nothing ever had before. I will never let go of what I have found." What God did for Kurt He can do for anyone else who asks Him. That's what theology is all about—changed lives.

Keep learning. Keep growing. Keep a blessed stubbornness in your resolve to serve Christ. God bless you as you live your faith in everyday life.

NOTES

Introduction

1. C. S. Lewis, *The Joyful Christian* (New York: Simon and Schuster, 1977), 34.

Chapter 2

1. Eleanor Doan, *The Complete Speaker's Sourcebook,* 2 vols. (Grand Rapids: Zondervan Publishing House, 1996), 2:74.

2. Wayne Martindale and Jerry Root, eds., *The Quotable Lewis* (Wheaton, Ill.: Tyndale House Publishers, 1963), 34.

Chapter 3

1. Doan, *Complete Speaker's Sourcebook,* 2:75.

Chapter 4

1. Martindale and Root, *Quotable Lewis,* 101.

Chapter 5

1. Doan, *Complete Speaker's Sourcebook,* 2:312.
2. Ibid., 76.

Chapter 6

1. Billy Hughey and Joyce Hughey, *A Rainbow of Hope* (El Reno, Okla.: Rainbow Studies, 1994), 23.
2. Doan, *Complete Speaker's Sourcebook,* 1:125.
3. Ibid., 2:205.
4. Ibid.

Chapter 7

1. Doan, *Complete Speaker's Sourcebook,* 2:188.
2. Ibid., 1:118.

Chapter 8

1. *The Quotable Bresee,* ed. Harold Ivan Smith (Kansas City: Beacon Hill Press of Kansas City, 1983), 186.
2. Hughey and Hughey, *Rainbow of Hope,* 111.

Chapter 9

1. Cort R. Flint, ed., *The Quotable Billy Graham* (Anderson, S.C.: Droke House Publishers, 1966), 93.
2. Doan, *Complete Speaker's Sourcebook,* 2:153.
3. Hughey and Hughey, *Rainbow of Hope,* 123.

Chapter 10

1. John Wesley, *The Works of John Wesley,* 3rd ed., 14 vols. (reprint, Kansas City: Beacon Hill Press of Kansas City, 1978-79), 5:57.

Chapter 11
1. Wesley, *Works*, 6:68.
2. Albert F. Harper, ed., *The Wesley Bible* (Nashville: Thomas Nelson Publishers, 1990), 1748.

Chapter 12
1. John Wesley, *The Works of John Wesley*, 3rd ed., vol. 12 (Grand Rapids: Baker Book House, 1979), 9.

Chapter 14
1. Smith, *Quotable Bresee*, 34.
2. Stevens W. Anderson, ed., *Compact Classics*, vol. 3 (Salt Lake City: Lan C. England, 1994), 433.
3. Ibid., 434.
4. Ibid., 441.
5. Hughey and Hughey, *Rainbow of Hope*, 40.
6. Smith, *Quotable Bresee*, 35.

Chapter 16
1. Smith, *Quotable Bresee*, 93.
2. Hughey and Hughey, *Rainbow of Hope*, 247.
3. Doan, *Complete Speaker's Sourcebook*, 2:88.

Chapter 19
1. Anderson, *Compact Classics*, 3:431.
2. Smith, *Quotable Bresee*, 82.

Chapter 20
1. Anderson, *Compact Classics*, 3:447.

Chapter 21
1. Alex Ayers, ed., *The Wit and Wisdom of Mark Twain* (New York: Harper and Row, 1987), 6.
2. Flint, *Quotable Billy Graham*, 70.
3. Smith, *Quotable Bresee*, 80.

Chapter 25
1. Friedrich von Logau, trans. Henry Wadsworth Longfellow in "Retribution."
2. Stevens W. Anderson, ed., *Compact Classics*, vol. 1 (Salt Lake City: Lan C. England, 1991), 183.

Chapter 27
1. C. S. Lewis, *The Great Divorce* (New York: Macmillan Co., 1946), 72-73.

Chapter 28
1. Anderson, *Compact Classics*, 3:436.

GLOSSARY

Angels—heavenly messengers sent from God to work with individuals or circumstances on the earth.

Anthropological Argument—an argument for the existence of God that says Someone gave us our built-in awareness that we ought to do the right thing.

Atonement—Christ brought the Holy Father and sinful humanity together through His sacrificial death on the Cross.

Attributes of God—qualities or concepts that attempt to define or describe who God is and how He relates to His creation. We always remember that He is beyond, above, and more than all categories of human language and understanding.

Authority of Scripture—the Bible represents the final authority for Christians in presenting God's will and having the right to define what we should believe and how we should live.

Baptism—the outward sign that symbolizes God washing our sins away as we die with Christ in a water grave and are resurrected to new spiritual life.

Christian Ethics—they deal with the lifestyle choices Christians make as they live their commitment to Jesus Christ at home and in the marketplace.

Church—the Body of Believers who confess Jesus Christ as the Son of God and trust in Him for salvation. It unites together under Christ's leadership and is His hands and feet to do His work on earth.

Communion—literally means "fellowship" or "participation" and is another name for the Lord's Supper.

Conscience—the internal moral compass that God placed within humanity that points toward God and right.

Conversion—the combination of activities or events that transforms a sinner into a child of God. It includes a repentant heart, forgiveness of sins, justification in God's sight, new birth, adoption into God's family, and the witness of the Spirit or assurance.

Cosmological Argument—an argument for the existence of God that says Someone put everything into motion in our world.

Creation—God brought everything that exists into being by His creative word, including the earth and everything on it, and space and everything in it.

Deity of Christ—during His earthly ministry, Christ remained fully divine, the second Person of the Trinity.

Dichotomy—the division of human beings into two parts—physical and spiritual.

Dualism—the false belief that God and Satan are balanced powers in the battle between good and evil.

Entire Sanctification—it begins with a deeper surrender or consecration of a believer to God's will and an invitation for Him to take charge of the control center of life, continues with faith and trust that God accepts our consecration, and is received as an undeserved gift from God.

Eschatology—the doctrine of last things that deals with my personal end on earth and the end of the world as we know it.

Eternal Life—begins the moment a person accepts Jesus Christ as personal Savior and continues forever and ever in heaven. It is the completion of salvation and involves living a life filled with and growing in righteousness, holiness, love, joy, goodness, and all the other attributes of God that He shares with us.

Eternity—the endless succession of time as it stretches earthly time out for ever and ever.

Eucharist—literally means "giving thanks" and is another name for the Lord's Supper.

Faith Glasses—the Spirit of God gives Christians clear vision to see things from His perspective and strive toward His excellence.

General Revelation—clues or signposts of God's existence found in nature, human religious hunger, and recorded history.

Growth in Grace—the growth and development in the faith that has spiritual maturity and Christlikeness as its goal.

Heaven—the dwelling place of God and His followers; it is a constant state of completion, satisfaction, and fulfillment in the unhindered presence of God.

Hell—the absence of the presence of God and a place where the damned suffer loneliness, hopelessness, the mental torment of past decisions, and the way they mistreated people and God.

Holy Spirit—the fully divine third Person of the Trinity along with the Father and Son; His most significant work today is in bringing us God's presence and taking our thoughts and prayers back to the Father.

Humanity of Christ—during His earthly ministry, Christ had a physical body and experienced the usual physical limitations like hunger, thirst, and fatigue; He had a human psychological and emotional makeup and experienced the full range of human emotions.

Human Nature—the common nature of humans that defines them as humans prior to making any personal choices.

Image of God in Humanity—God created humanity something like himself in the areas of reasoning ability, social ability, moral ability, creative ability, responsibility, and spirituality.

Immanence of God—God immanently involves himself in earthly life and works quietly behind the scenes to help humanity and address earthly needs.

Inspiration of Scripture—the Bible contains an extraordinary message divinely given to human writers in supernatural ways so that the material, energized by the Holy Spirit, inspires readers toward God and spiritual matters when they read it.

Judgment Day—following the second coming of Christ and the bodily resurrection of everyone who has ever lived on earth. Christ will sit in the seat of judgment and everyone, both righteous and unrighteous, will appear before Him for final judgment. Those who had faith in Christ as Savior will stand on His right, and those who rejected Him on His left. Satan and demons will also receive their final judgment on that day.

Justification—Christ's sacrificial death on the Cross enables the Father to see us through eyes of grace and mercy; He declares us free from the guilt and penalty of our past sins and gives us a new start. He also makes us righteous as He empowers us by His grace to do what is right.

Lordship—God sets the bounds within which everything in creation operates.

Lord's Supper—the memorial of Christ's sacrificial death on the Cross, with the bread representing the body of Christ and the juice His blood, and a reminder of His coming again. Also know as Communion or the Eucharist.

Means of Grace—the channels of God's grace in daily life. They include prayer, Bible reading, meditation, corporate worship, the Lord's Supper, Christian fellowship, fasting, discipline, service, and suffering.

Millennium—means 1,000 and refers to either the literal belief in Christ's millennial rule on earth with His saints prior to the end of the world and the final Judgment or to the figurative belief in the growth of the kingdom of God through the Church from Bible times until the end of the world or to the reign of Christ eternally in heaven.

Moral Evil—the results of harmful choices made by people, like war, crime, and drunk-driving accidents.

Natural Evil—the destructive forces of nature, like tornadoes, earthquakes, and hurricanes, or the destructive forces of diseases, like cancer, diabetes, and heart disease.

Omnipotence—God possesses ability to use His will to do anything consistent with His nature.

Omnipresence—God knows all the facts and possesses perfect understanding to make correct decisions every time.

Ontological Argument—an argument for the existence of God that says Someone gave us our ability to think about the greatest and highest and best that we can conceive.

Original Sin—the universal and hereditary sinfulness of all humanity resulting from Adam and Eve's selfish use of free will in the Garden of Eden.

Prayer—personal communication between humanity and God.

Predestination—the eternal destiny of any who accept God's plan of salvation through the sacrifice of Christ on the Cross is guaranteed. It does not determine who gets picked for salvation but rather tells what happens to those who accept God's salvation offer.

Prevenient Grace—the grace that goes before and includes all God graciously does before we get saved to bring us to the point of salvation.

Providence—God actively preserves and sustains our world and directs it toward His desired end and personally works in our lives.

Regeneration—another name for the new birth that happens the moment a person repents and has faith in Jesus Christ. It restores our relationship with God.

Repentance—it involves getting honest with yourself and with God about sin, being truly sorry for your ways, confessing your condition to God, and changing your mind and behavior about sinful actions and attitudes.

Resurrection of Christ—the Father brought Jesus Christ back to life after His crucifixion and validated the claims of His ministry; resurrection power became the energizing force for evangelization and the nurture of the Early Church.

Saving Faith—an intellectual, psychological, emotional, and spiritual resolve to believe and live the truth of the gospel message as presented in the New Testament.

Satan—the word means "adversary" or "deceiver." He is a personal being who is in revolt against God and deceives people about the truth of God, encourages disobedience against God, hinders followers of God, and seeks to destroy God's kingdom on earth.

Second Coming of Christ—the same Jesus who lived on earth will personally revisit earth, accompanied by a great host of heavenly angels. He will appear in the eastern sky and will be visible to everyone. His return will signal the glorious triumph of God's good plans for the world and will mark the end of time as we know it.

Sin—a willful transgression of God's known law; missing the mark. Technically, wrongdoing performed in ignorance is sometimes also classified as sin, but practically an act or attitude is normally judged by God as sin based on a willful motive and intention to transgress.

Sin's Consequences—the list includes God's displeasure, guilt, shame, hiding both from others and self, restless and dissatisfied spirit, bondage, and spiritual, physical, and eternal death.

Sovereign—God has the absolute right to rule His creation as He sees fit.

Special Revelation—detailed information about God found in the life and ministry of Jesus Christ and the Bible given for the purpose of opening a way for intimate friendship with God.

Systemic Evil—the effects of human rebellion against God that work their way into the social, political, and religious systems of the world.

Teleological Argument—an argument for the existence of God that says Someone gave purpose, order, and intelligent direction to all things in our world.

Theocracy—the form of government that God desired for Israel whereby they looked to Him for leadership.

Total Depravity—sin affects humanity's entire being—body, mind, reason, emotion, and will—so that people are inclined toward self, leaving them with neither the will, the desire, nor the ability to find God's favor.

Transcendence of God—God is above and beyond all we know and can work in miraculous ways to meet human needs or address earthly concerns.

Tribulation—a time of intense suffering and persecution at the end of time on earth.

Trichotomy—the division of human beings into three parts—physical, soul, spirit.

Trinity—the Christian understanding of our One God as represented in the three Persons of Father, Son, and Holy Spirit.

Virgin Conception—God's miraculous activity in placing Jesus in Mary's body without her having sexual activity with either man or God.

Witness of the Spirit (direct)—the assurance of God's Spirit to our spirit that God has accepted our repentant heart, forgives us of our sins, justifies us in His sight, grants us new birth, and adopts us into His family.

Witness of the Spirit (indirect)—people watch our lives following conversion and see the evidence of God working within us, and we see the difference as well.

WORKS CITED*

Anderson, Stevens W., ed. *Compact Classics*. Vol. 1. Salt Lake City: Lan C. England, 1991.

———. *Compact Classics*. Vol. 2. Salt Lake City: Lan C. England, 1993.

———. *Compact Classics*. Vol. 3. Salt Lake City: Lan C. England, 1994.

Ayers, Alex, ed. *The Wit and Wisdom of Mark Twain*. New York: Harper and Row, 1987.

Buechner, Frederick. *Wishful Thinking: A Theological ABC*. New York: Harper and Row, 1973.

Doan, Eleanor. *The Complete Speaker's Sourcebook*. Vols. 1 and 2. Grand Rapids: Zondervan Publishing House, 1996.

Flint, Cort R., ed. *The Quotable Billy Graham*. Anderson, S.C.: Droke House Publishers, 1966.

Harper, Albert F., ed. *The Wesley Bible*. Nashville: Thomas Nelson Publishers, 1990.

Hearth, Amy Hill. *The Delany Sisters' Book of Everyday Wisdom*. New York: Kodansha International, 1994.

Hughey, Billy, and Joyce Hughey. *A Rainbow of Hope*. El Reno, Okla.: Rainbow Studies, 1994.

Kennedy, Gerald. *A Reader's Notebook*. New York: Harper and Brothers, 1953.

Lewis, C. S. *The Great Divorce*. (New York: Macmillan Co., 1946).

———. *The Joyful Christian*. New York: Simon and Schuster, 1977.

———. *Miracles*. New York: Macmillan, 1960.

Martindale, Wayne, and Jerry Root, eds. *The Quotable Lewis*. Wheaton, Ill.: Tyndale House Publishers, 1963.

Smith, Harold Ivan, ed. *The Quotable Bresee*. Kansas City: Beacon Hill Press of Kansas City, 1983.

Wesley, John. *The Works of John Wesley*. 3rd ed. Vols. 5, 6, and 11. Kansas City: Beacon Hill Press of Kansas City, 1978-79.

Wesley, John. *The Works of John Wesley*. 3rd ed. Vol 12. Grand Rapids: Baker Book House, 1979.

---

*In this volume and in *Coffee Shop Theology*.

INDEX

BECAUSE KNOWING WHAT YOU BELIEVE IS IMPORTANT . . .

Always be prepared to give an answer to everyone who asks you to give the reason for the hope that you have.

— Peter 3:15*b*

More than ever before, Christians must know what we believe and why. The reason is simple but serious. In a world where most ways of thinking are considered equally true regardless of how unscriptural they may be or how odd they may sound, if our anchor isn't set in a rock solid theology, we'll be washed out to sea on the riptide of bogus beliefs.

This first book in the Coffee Shop Theology set explains theological concepts and brings them into focus for everyday living. In *Coffee Shop Theology* Dr. Frank Moore covers a wide array of theological concepts and brings them by the "digestible" handfuls into your living room. Don't be turned off by the word "theology." Dr. Moore has left all the big words in the fat books.

Some of the concepts covered in this book:

The existence of God	Human nature
The Trinity	Sin
Angels	The virgin conception
God's self-revelation	The deity of Christ
Satan and demons	The Resurrection
The problem of evil	